Technical Bowhunting
The Ultimate Guide to Shooting Performance
By Joe Bell

Disclaimer

Please note that the publisher and author of this instructional book are NOT RESPONSIBLE in any manner whatsoever for any injury that may occur by reading and/or following the instructions herein.

It is essential that before following any of the activities, physical or otherwise, herein described, the reader or readers should first consult his or her physician for advice on whether or not the reader or readers should embark on the physical activity described herein. Since the physical activities described herein may be too sophisticated in nature, it is essential that a physician be consulted.

c/o APG Media • P.O. Box 15159
N. Hollywood, CA 91615-9268
Tel: (866) 834-1249 Fax: (818) 487-4550
www.up-publications.com

ISBN: 0-86568-266-6

Library of Congress Control Number: 2008903103

Editor: Dave Cater

Book Design: Suzanne K. Miller

Photography: Joe Bell, Darin Cooper, John Dudley, Easton Technical Products, Mathews Inc., Angelo Nogara and Hoyt USA.

TECHNICAL BOWHUNTING

The Ultimate Guide to Shooting Performance

BY JOE BELL

Contents

Section 1 – Insights for Maximum Performance

Section 2 — Pro-Level Shooting Technique

Section 3 — Specialized Advice

DEDICATION

To my wife, Krista, who has blessed me in so many ways, and to my daughters, Mikaela and Marissa, for making my life complete.

ACKNOWLEDGMENTS

I would like to thank those who were instrumental in the development of this book. Without their expert help, this project would lack true substance. These folks include Chuck Adams, Bruce Barrie, Darin Cooper, John Dudley, Rodney Huffman, David Kronengold, Bob Mizek, Angelo Nogara, Derek Phillips, Carl Pugliese, Mike Slinkard, Scott Shultz, Tim Strickland, Randy Ulmer, Ron Way, and Craig Yehle. Darin Cooper, Mike Slinkard and Randy Ulmer deserve special thanks for proofreading this book. Without their brilliant eyes, technical errors would've gone unnoticed.

Also, my deepest gratitude goes to my special bowhunting friends who make this sport so meaningful, thought provoking and enjoyable. They include Art Cain, Roy Cole, the Comptons, CJ Davis, Chris Denham, David Eder, Eric Fundum, Steve Galentine, Kevin Kaiser, David Kleist, Jeff Letherer, Dean MacDonald, Angelo Nogara, Carl Pugliese, Bill Ramsey, PJ Selinski and Ron Way.

To Bob Fromme for all his archery help over the years.

And, to all of those industry folks and advertisers who have supported my work over the years—you know who you are—thank you very much, too.

Last but certainly not least; I would like to thank God for giving me his strength.

INTRODUCTION

Author Joe Bell with a great Nevada mule deer, which he harvested during a wilderness-backpacking trip.

Back in the early 1980s, I began seriously shooting a compound bow and, shortly thereafter, took up bowhunting big game. Those beginning years were some of the most cherished moments in my life. I was taken aback by the cool look of a "wheeled" bow, especially one spray-painted in dull, drab-green camouflage. The entire event of shooting an arrow was captivating to me, and before I knew it I was thoroughly hooked on the sport. I did my best bowhunting nearly year 'round, whether in the rugged mountains close to home for deer, the deserts for small game, or the wild lands of Catalina and Santa Cruz Islands for exotics and wild boar. If the hunting license, tag and hunt didn't cost too much, I did everything I could to get myself there.

As a pretty serious gun hunter, this primitive way of being in the woods felt like a natural progression and, over time, it proved a more valuable fit. I appreciated the idea of carrying my weapon, hunting at peak hours, and then quietly stump-shooting my way back to camp. In over 20 years, I've never stopped exercising my passion for the sport. My motivation for shooting a bow and bowhunting has been running like wild fire.

In those early years, I shot like a mad man, to the point of breaking down muscles. Slowly I figured out how many arrows I could shoot without hurting my shooting muscles and rotator cuff. When visiting friends or family, my bow went with me. I enjoyed weeknight league, and shot 3-Ds occasionally on the weekends. When I hunted, I went at it as hard as I could, like a predator on the prowl, intent on the kill. Bowhunting was no longer a hobby; it became a part of who I was. Deep down I was becoming a bowhunter for life.

Despite all this, whether I was practicing or hunting, improvement was always apparent. To shoot accurately, or to ambush game, it became all about pushing beyond normal limits, always. I became discouraged at times, but for some reason these mental challenges just drew me in, more and more. Like any laborer to his craft, I had to beat 'em.

That's when problems began to arise. Specifically, I began placing more and more pressure on myself to shoot better, particularly when hunting. I wanted to perform like a machine, not make mistakes. After all, I shot so much I shouldn't have any faults, or so I thought. Naturally, this mindset proved counterproductive, and eventually I adopted some dreaded shooting habits, which caused me years of despair.

Fortunately, being hardheaded, I willed myself to succeed and eventually turned for help. I read every book and magazine article out there that I could get my hands on, trying to find answers to my questions and solutions for my problems. Some of this reading proved worthwhile, but mostly I found myself becoming more frustrated. In most cases, I found only shreds of helpful pointers that I thought might improve my shooting technique and teach me a bit more about equipment set-up and selection. I was a serious enthusiast, looking for expert advice. This was hard to come by.

At times I got lucky and was given some good guidance from accomplished bowhunters, but mostly I learned the hard way—through trial and error.

In the end, there were plenty of "gaps" in my learning curve, and I continued to feel frustrated with my progression in the sport, mostly because I was still occasionally blowing "easy" shots on big game. I wanted to improve, at a much faster rate than the one I was going at.

In many ways, this prompted my ambition and involvement in the archery industry. Bowhunting, and hunting in general, inspired me to not only pursue a career in outdoor writing but also to continue my neverending search for the truths behind the best techniques, best equipment, and pretty much best anything else that relates to the sport I love. Step by step, I found myself drawing closer and closer to this goal. I was slowly gaining lots of valuable tools that eventually made me much more confident, both as a shooter and bowhunter.

While learning, one thing stood out about the process: it was the smaller details that seemed to make a significant difference to my success.

Today, after years of serious shooting, bowhunting, in-depth testing, reviewing, experimentation, and heavy involvement in the industry speaking with archery pros, coaches and equipment designers, I've learned a wealth of valuable information. I now have a firm grasp on the most important fundamentals in bowhunting. My desire in writing this book is to pass this information on to you, with the hope that it will elevate your success just as it has with mine.

This is the main inspiration behind *Technical Bowhunting*—to share what I personally know to be beneficial in bowhunting, and giving you the insights and truths that I've learned from some of the industry's best.

Please don't take me wrong; I'm not this "premier" bowhunter with all of the answers. I'm still learning just like any level of archer.

Perhaps the most important element to acknowledge in any sport, or life matter, is that we never stop learning. I do believe, however, that by bringing together a spectrum of authoritative influences in one written body I am trying to take you as close to bowhunting greatness as possible. I have taken the counsel from a handful of bowhunters that I know, admire and deeply respect and have sprinkled their knowledge and excellence throughout the book. Perhaps this is what makes *Technical Bowhunting* unique. It's a compilation of many authoritative voices, not just mine. This is why it can aid and educate you in a potent, meaningful, and well-rounded fashion. It is unlike any other source you will find.

If the things in this book help you half as much as they have helped me, I will be very pleased. In the end, I believe you'll soar to incredible new heights and enjoy the sport more than ever before. Here's to a long-lasting pursuit dotting the "X" and to taking home that nice bowhunting trophy.

Regards,

Joe Bell

BY JOE BELL

FOREWORD

Chuck Adams is America's best-known bowhunter. His books and magazine articles have inspired countless bowhunters over the last three decades, including the author.

I suspected that Joe Bell was one of the good guys the first time we talked. The year was 1998, and Joe had just become Editor of *Bow & Arrow Hunting* magazine. What would normally have been a short, brass-tacks telephone conversation between a long-time writer for that publication and a new editor became a long and enthusiastic chat about bowhunting and archery gear. Even at age 26, Joe Bell displayed knowledge of hunting archery that impressed me.

My suspicions were confirmed as the years went by. At an archery trade show shortly after Joe became editor, we had dinner and talked. It took us a few minutes to hammer out column and feature assignments for the year, and then we switched to a topic that was clearly more important to both of us—hunting big game with a bow. This did not feel like a business dinner at all. It was more like two old hunting pals comparing stories and ideas about their favorite and all-consuming sport. I realized that night that Joe Bell ate, drank and slept bowhunting just as much as I did—a kindred spirit thoroughly jazzed about archery, wildlife, and the great outdoors.

Unlike many editors, writers, and archery manufacturers I have encountered during my 35-year bowhunting career, Joe Bell is a hunter first and a writer second. Please do not mistake my meaning. He is very good at both. But the spark so often missing in "career archers" is burning bright in Joe. He has always been intensely curious about bows, arrows and other technical archery gear. This intensity stems from his desire to shoot better, and bag more game, than he did the year before.

Joe Bell's job as the editor of a major archery magazine has helped tremendously in this quest. He has unfettered access to the latest ideas from archery experts and the latest testing materials from cutting-edge manufacturers and engineers. He spends many hours each week discussing archery with top shooters and testing theories and products. This is his job, certainly, but it is also his passion.

As you begin to read this excellent book, you will discover that Joe Bell has a well-polished skill to pass along ideas clearly and simply in print. And I can promise that Joe knows what he is talking about. For me, reading *Technical Bowhunting* was much like my many conversations with Joe over the years. The enthusiasm is there, and so is deep, practical knowledge about how every bowhunter can be a better shot on game. This is not a theoretical, half-B.S. discussion by some self-proclaimed armchair expert. *Technical Bowhunting* is the real deal.

I like the way this book is written and organized. If you digest it chapter by chapter, you will find it to be a complete blueprint to improving your ability to shoot animals with a bow. Joe does not confuse pure target archery with bowhunting—a mistake commonly made by "shooting elites" on the tournament circuit. Punching bull's-eyes and nailing critters are worlds apart, and Joe makes this distinction abundantly clear. He certainly taps the expertise of archers who are good on targets *and* game. But the emphasis is game. *Technical Bowhunting* is a pleasant mix of interviews with experts and Joe's own knowledge of our sport.

From arrow speed to broadhead selection to shooting form, this is a book for the serious hunter. It is also a book for anyone who wants to be self-sufficient at archery, with excellent information on maintaining and improving modern archery gear. If you've ever been plagued by buck fever, or torn your hair out over a poorly tuned bow, this is the book for you. It solves problems.

If you prefer to win indoor archery contests or wish to badmouth better bowhunting shots instead of improving your own skill, I suggest you lay this volume aside. Joe's goal is improving your deadly ability on deer, elk, bear, and other species. Read with an open mind, and you will improve.

Joe Bell has been a rising star in archery for more than a decade, and I am honored to write this foreword for his book. In many ways, our paths have been the same. Both of us fell in love with bowhunting as teenagers. Both of us began our editorial careers in Southern California—a great professional environment, perhaps, but a terrible place to be an avid bowhunter. After establishing ourselves, we both left the bright lights for greener bowhunting pastures. I moved to Wyoming, and Joe moved to Arizona—both excellent places to write and chase animals.

Joe remains Editor for *Bow & Arrow Hunting* magazine, and now has javelina, Coues deer, mule deer, elk, and antelope in his backyard. Good for him. I am proud of his accomplishments in the archery industry, and I wish him well with this book. It is the reflection of a man—a man who understands the intricate ins and outs of accurately shooting a hunting bow. Read carefully, and you will learn a lot.

—Chuck Adams, 2008

Section 1

Insights for Maximum Performance

Chapter 1
Where Success Begins – Proper Shooting Form

Creating a Shooting System That's Easy to Duplicate

"First we form habits, then they form us. Conquer your bad habits or they will conquer you."
—Rob Gilbert

When shooting, comfort is of great importance, since your body must withstand the tension of the bow while you just focus on aiming and nothing else. *Note:* The archer's draw-side arm elbow is even or slightly above the arrow, which identifies proper technique.

The crowd's presence was unsettling as I stepped out to shoot. Plagued by intimidation, I could feel tiny amounts of sweat easing out of the pores on my usually dry hands as I methodically slid the carbon Easton ACC arrow down along the flipper rest, then eased it back ½ inch to clip the nock in place. *Focus…focus…* I kept telling myself, feeling the anxiety of the moment worsening by the second.

Firmly gripping the bowstring, I hit full draw and slowly planted the 45-yard hold on the McKenzie mule deer. I began to quiver. Emotions flooded in now, with the line between failure and success a cut and dry 50-50. Would I stay hooked up or lose control? This thought chipped away at what little confidence I had.

Then, the words I mentally chiseled into my psyche for months on end just before taking a shot echoed loudly within. *Aim…aim…aim.* Immediately, a calm feeling came over me that only a well-taught, well-practiced archer could comprehend. My bodily mechanics idled into motion.

In a moment, my whole body relaxed except for the muscles in my back, which progressively tightened, and as the bow's limbs sprung forward, my fingers slid back across my ear. "Man," some guy muttered in the crowd. "That was one heckuva shot." I stood there, still in classic follow-through position with my bow arm pointed at the target, stunned, like I was jolted out of a daydream.

Pressure-related shots can quickly destroy a shooter, unless you have the right mental armor. The key to performing well comes from immersing yourself in the shooting process, like I somehow did on that 3-D shot. I'm not my best in the face of pressure, but when a process becomes ingrained, second nature so to speak, each step in the cycle equals a predictable, consistent outcome.

Shooting in a clutch situation can be frightening—you'll feel anxiety tightening its grasp— but as a bowhunter or 3-D archer, inevitably you'll find yourself in this situation. The key to top performance under such scenarios is to adopt a shooting system easily duplicated from shot to shot, regardless of the circumstances.

To learn the process, you must be willing to drop old habits to learn new ones. It takes work, patience and even possibly some expert coaching, but once the work is done, you'll start punching bull's-eyes and bagging critters like you've never done before. I suggest paying now in the form of dedication and attention to proper shooting technique so that you are sure to reap the positive results later.

Fact: Repeatable Technique Dictates Good Shooting Form

Step 1

Step 2

Step 3

Step 4

When shooting, be methodical, making sure each step is carried out the same way from one shot to the next. This allows your subconscious mind to absorb the necessary steps behind a properly executed shot. This promotes consistency, and results in great accuracy.

10 Steps to Perfect Form

Of course, experts' opinions vary widely on the best techniques, but all successful archers agree that the shooting process *must* be consistent. In other words, it is imperative that you choose a method that is easily copied so you can theoretically perform the same on every shot. Here are my most-foolproof methods.

No. 1: Stance

Most archers put little thought into their stance, however, a solid stance is fundamental to shooting well. A slightly open stance (as shown here), with your feet a shoulder-width apart, is a widely used stance. However, some archers prefer a closed stance (tips of toes 90 degrees to target). *Note:* The tip of the arrow is pointed at the target.

Stance is at the core of good shooting form; in other words, how you position your feet in relation to the target. The best shooting stance is comfortable and solid. For maximum stability, place your feet about a shoulder-width apart, with your body's weight equally distributed between the rear and midsection of the feet.

Most experts recommend a slightly open stance, which constitutes positioning your toes 90 degrees to the target, then taking a half-step backward with the foot closest to the target. This stance places your chest more toward the target, which allows for greater bowstring clearance along the chest and bow arm.

However, not every archer will prefer this stance. To fine-tune your stance simply close your eyes and draw your bow (without an arrow, of course), and anchor as you normally would. Now move your body around, shifting your feet in the most stable, comfortable spot. Then open your eyes and mark the direction of your aim. Let down, then reference the position of your feet by taking an arrow and pointing it straight at the aiming spot. That's your stance.

No. 2: Proper Bow Grip

A relaxed bow hand is essential to eliminate torque, which can cause accuracy problems, particularly with broadheads.

The variable here is hand torque, so you want to position your hand on the grip in a way that will make it as torque-free as possible.

Randy Ulmer, a past pro-champion target/3-D archer and renowned bowhunter, suggests holding your hand out as if you were going to grip the bow, keeping it fairly rigid as if pressure was on it. Next, take your thumb from your other hand and push into your bow-hand palm at various locations. Every spot you press on will cause your hand to move or collapse in position, except for one location, and that's where you want to place the pressure of the bow's grip. This location happens to be where your forearm bones dead end into the base of your palm, so it represents a bone-to-bone contact point. It's the most reliable and most torque-resistant way to shoot a bow.

To position my hand on the grip, I like to grab the bow's grip using only my thumb and index finger, keeping my hand and thumb pointed at a slight outward angle (the most relaxed posture). From here, I begin pulling on the string, and allow my fingers to relax. You can either keep the other three fingers "tucked into" the grip or loosely dangle them in a comfortable position.

Beyond this, the secret to a torque-free hand is to make sure it's comfortable and completely relaxed. Essentially, at this point, it should view the job as dead weight. Your fingers or palm shouldn't move one smidgen until the arrow impacts the target.

No. 3: Drawing the Bow

1.   2.

3.   4.

When drawing the bow, ideally you should keep the bow hand pointed at the target as you maintain a high elbow throughout the process. This will effectively transfer the weight of the bow to your back muscles for increased strength and string pressure.

This may seem inconsequential but drawing the bow properly does one vitally important thing: it transfers the drawing tension to your back muscles, which are large and strong and will allow you to hold steady during the shot.

Drawing the bow properly is simple. Think of your draw-arm elbow following the motion similar to a turning wheel. With your elbow pivoted about as high as your jaw line or mouth, pull on the bowstring with your elbow following a half-circle movement. This will effectively transfer the bow's tension to your rhomboid muscles (which are in your back between the shoulder blades). From here, you can relax the rest of your body and let these hardy muscles take care of triggering the shot *(more on this later)*.

I see a lot of archers drawing the bow with their elbow low and to the side. When done this way, your arm and bicep muscles take on the drawing weight, not your back muscles.

No. 4: Bow-Arm Position

A low and locked bow-arm shoulder utilizes the least amount of muscle tension. This promotes steadier aiming.

When you hold steady, shooting becomes more comfortable and non-intimidating. The end result is tighter arrow groups. The opposite holds true when you don't aim well. You become more of a "snap-shooter" as the pin weaves in and out of the bull's-eye, and eventually shooting problems of all sorts begin to arise.

A strong, relaxed bow arm is one key to aiming steady. To achieve this, keep your draw-side shoulder low, down and in a locked position. This approach eliminates as much muscle tension as possible. Simply put, flex a muscle and you have discomfort and ultimately a shaky aim.

"One discipline always leads to another discipline."
—Jim Rohn

To recognize a relaxed, low, locked bow-arm, stand up, hold your hand up at 90 degrees as if holding a bow. Notice the position of your shoulder. Now, try and roll your shoulder in and out. When it's out (now closer to your chin), you are involving muscle movement. When it's down, you are allowing this joint to naturally lock into a bone-to-bone location, which is easy to duplicate from shot to shot since no muscles are involved. And with no muscle flex, there's no struggle or quiver. Try it for a week or two and you'll quickly notice the aiming advantage.

Note: A low, locked bow-arm shoulder is easiest to achieve by bending at the waist and leaning slightly forward as you point the bow at the target and begin drawing the bow back.

No. 5: Draw Length and Draw Weight

Darin Cooper illustrates proper draw length and shot anchor. Correct draw length means your head must maintain a natural position, as if you're just looking straight ahead, not with the nose pointed up or down. Also, establish a solid anchor, but don't force the bowstring too hard into the face, which can torque the string differently on each shot, resulting in left and right arrow impacts.

You must be relaxed and comfortable to shoot with proper form. The key is correct bow fit, with proper draw length and weight as the essential elements.

Draw Length: To achieve your "rough" draw length, the wingspan method works pretty well. You simply stand with your back against a wall—arms spread out—while a friend measures your middle fingertip (on one hand) to the other hand's middle fingertip. You take this measurement and divide it by 2.5. For example, if your arm span measures 70 inches, your draw length is roughly 28 inches (i.e., 70 inches divided by 2.5 = 28).

I say "rough" measurement because a string loop and release-aid choice can alter this draw length.

With today's ultra short axle-to-axle bows, proper draw length is becoming more complicated, mostly because veteran shooters like to position the string lightly against the middle of the nose while anchored solidly at full draw. With shorter bows, the string angle is more acute and a bit longer draw length is needed to bring this string back in closer to the shooter's nose tip. The alternative is to tilt your face and nose downward, which isn't the best choice since it can create comfort problems, compared to using a relaxed, naturally upright head position.

I've found the best way to remedy short-bow string angle is to use one of the newer short nose release-aids, such as the Scott Wildcat or Jim Fletcher Flathead, which are designed to increase your draw length by ¼-to-½ inch. You can increase your draw-length by that much and place the bowstring closer in to your nose.

For example, when I shoot a 33-to-37-inch axle-to-axle bow, I use a 27-inch draw using a Scott Little Bitty Goose NCS release. When switching to a shorter 30- or 31-inch bow, I use a 27 ¼-to-27 ½-inch draw length using a Scott Wildcat NCS or Sabertooth NCS release. I anchor both bows by placing my hand along my jawbone and with the bowstring just barely touching my nose tip. Either way, my head is tilted naturally forward, not downward or upward, and my shooting form remains as relaxed and comfortable as possible.

One good indicator of correct draw length is noting the alignment of your draw-arm elbow. It should be more or less in line with the arrow and the target, not left or right.

If you don't want to switch release-aids, your best bet is to choose a bow that offers the ideal string angle based on your draw-length and face position.

Darin Cooper, senior product design engineer for Hoyt USA, explains that to find the correct bow-axle length, an archer should stand erect facing forward with only the bow and not the head pointed to the target. He says to draw the bow to the approximate anchor point and then rotate the head toward the target. The string should be in close proximity to the tip of the archer's nose without having to move his head fore and aft or tilt it up or down. This assumes the rest of the archer's form is correct.

As a general rule, longer-draw archers typically require longer axle-to-axle bows to maintain their natural posture and shooting form for maximum accuracy. Shorter-draw archers can typically shoot shorter axle bows more comfortably.

Short-draw shooters can get by with longer axle-to-axle bows, if they wish, by using and lengthening or shortening the size of a shooting loop to adjust how the angle of the string crosses their face.

Draw Weight: As far as draw weight goes, use common sense. Proper draw weight is identified as any pull-weight you can draw back smoothly from nearly any position. A good test is to sit in a chair with your legs open and the bow positioned in the middle of your legs at arm's length. Now draw the bow back while keeping the bow straight out in front of you. If you can't draw back fairly smoothly, then you're shooting too much draw weight.

When drawing the bow back, it's important to make a habit out of raising the bow no more than 4-to-6 inches above your line of sight. This not only allows proper drawing form so you can "load up" your back muscles, but it also allows less bow movement when drawing down on animals while hunting.

Fact: A Smooth Pull From Any Position Defines Proper Draw Weight

---

No. 6: Shot Anchor

Again, this is where consistency really counts. Place your shooting hand somewhere along the side of your face where it can be supported by your jawbone. It must stay unwavering as you release the trigger on the release or smoothly relax your fingers to free the bowstring. This will minimize or eliminate horizontal torque. Once you find a comfortable, solid place to support your hand, adjust the peep accordingly. Remember, ideally your face should be naturally straight, not up or down, as you look through the peep.

The most common anchor for a release shooter using a wrist-strap release is to create a "V" with the web of the thumb and index finger, and use it to press against the jawbone, that portion in line and in front of the bottom of the ear. Then place the nose so it just touches the tip of the bowstring, with the peep perfectly in line.

Some archers draw a little further back, using the knuckle of their index finger and pressing it against the "valley" just below the ear lobe.

Most pro archers recommend a light touch against the face. I say, use whatever anchor breeds consistency. A great way to examine your anchor point is to look in the mirror and see if the bowstring is compressed against your face. If it is, string torque can occur and you can bet each time you shoot this force will vary, causing your arrows to fly and hit differently. An easy-to-duplicate anchor point is one of the most crucial, yet lightly talked about subjects in archery. Get it right.

No 7: T-Form

This is where you verify correct draw length and a comfortable, relaxed shooting position. When an archer shows proper "T" form, his body (when you look at his back) will be in a position that represents the shape of a "T." Let's start with the torso area. It should be naturally straight, so a straight line can be drawn through your spinal column. The horizontal line in the "T" represents your arms, from the bottom portion of your elbow and arm through the top of your bow-arm shoulder along the top of your arm and into the middle of your hand.

The key here is to have a high elbow point, about the height of your ears. This elbow position helps you to make full use of your back muscles, which allows you to hold the bow steady and comfortable. This is also vital for those who want to "trigger" the shot using their back muscles so they can achieve a surprise-type release.

No. 8: Aiming

How do you aim? Well, there isn't a right or wrong way. You can focus on the target and blur the sight pin, or just the opposite—focus on the sight pin and blur the target. Some pro-level shooters prefer to center their attention at the mid-way spot between the sight pin and target, so both are somewhat in focus.

Professional coach Tim Strickland says he's helped more people rid themselves of target panic (freezing off target) by focusing on the sight pin rather than the target. He says a lot of it comes down to your personality type, so you should experiment to see which method works best for you.

These photos illustrate proper "T" form. Imagine a vertical line through the archer's spinal column, with the horizontal line of the "T" representing the arms, from the bottom portion of your elbow and arm through the top of your bow-arm shoulder along the top of your arm and into the middle of your hand. Note how the draw-arm elbow is just above the arrow, and in line with the archer's nose.

It's important to maintain proper "T" form despite shooting upward or downward. To do this, twist at the waist.

Another important point to emphasize here is that once you start the draw, be sure to pre-aim somewhere near the target. This way, you can get on target quickly and smoothly swing your sight pin into the aiming circle or the animal's kill zone. Most coaches recommend that you pre-aim just above the aiming spot and smoothly come down on the aiming spot.

As a bowhunter, I've always found it more beneficial to pre-aim from below, slowly but smoothly bringing my sight pin up. This allows me to get on target faster when faced with a fleeing, close-range shot. In this case, when using a multiple-pin sight, my 20-yard pin comes into the kill first, not my 60-yard pin, so I'm less distracted and able to shoot faster.

However, coming in from above and down requires less muscle strain, so it could keep you more relaxed and steadier during the aim.

Well-known bowhunters Chuck Adams and Randy Ulmer come up on the target as well. Randy says if he had to teach someone, he'd tell them to come down on target, because it allows you to relax into the target rather than tighten muscles to come up to the target.

Also, many archers wonder whether they should keep both eyes open or one eye closed during the aiming process. Keeping both eyes open is perhaps most ideal for bowhunting, since it maximizes viewing brightness and your peripheral vision. However, if your aiming eye is not as strong as your non-aiming eye, it's

TECH TIPS

Warm Up!

It's always a good idea to stretch your muscles before regular shooting practice, particularly in cold weather. This will increase performance and prevent muscle tears or injuries, such as rotator cuff tendonitis (a common problem among archers). I recommend the Bowfit Archery Exerciser (www.bowfit.com). Made from extra-strong sport tubing, this simple device allows you to easily adjust pulling resistance. You can also use this tool for strength training, and since it's so light and compact, you can use it anywhere, whether watching TV or while traveling.

best to close the left eye if you're a right-handed shooter (opposite for left-hand). This will eliminate "blurry" or two-image viewing. Some shooters, regardless of eye dominance, still insist on closing the non-aiming eye. They say it gives them more of a "tunnel view" while aiming, which increases their concentration.

> *"The more you prepare, the luckier you appear."*
> —*Terry Josephson*

No. 9: The Release

Back tension is important for a surprise release. After the shot, examine the position of your bow-arm and release hand. When proper back tension is used, the bow tends to go slightly forward and to the left and the release hand will move rearward along your face.

The more arrows you shoot, the more important a surprise-type release becomes. As we train our minds to do something over and over, with intense redundancy, it becomes nearly impossible to direct this action using our conscious mind. The more we think about something (consciously), the more we'll botch the process. For example, take something as simple as driving your car to the store. We no longer think about turning the steering wheel much, or how much pressure we put on the brake or gas pedal. If we did, our driving would turn disastrous.

The same goes for shooting a bow. However, the task of shooting a bow is much more intricate compared to driving a car. The goal in a car is rather broad and singular; you simply drive to get somewhere and the mission stops there. But when shooting a bow, the goal is specific and there is a demand for repetitiveness: dot the "X" on the target or the kill zone or the 3-D target over and over. To not think about making a good shot becomes increasingly difficult the more you do it. This is why shot anticipation is the No. 1 problem in archery.

Professional archery coach Tim Strickland believes in using key muscles in your back to trigger the shot, rather than shooting on command.

To overcome this tendency means you'll have to diffuse it, which means thinking about something else rather than the shot, or the target, or not so much the location of your sight pin.

I've learned a lot from my friend and NFAA coach Tim Strickland. He maintains, "To shoot differently means you'll have to think differently." He suggests using your entire body to "trigger" the release rather than your conscious mind saying "now!" to fire the bow.

According to Strickland, "You should refuse the tendency to shoot just because the sight pin is where it's supposed to be." In reality, this means very little and does not guarantee a good hit. Without good follow-through, back tension, and comfortable, relaxed shooting, the arrow won't land in the spot anyway, he suggests. "It's an illusion, and don't believe it."

Instead, rely on your entire body to trigger and direct the arrow accordingly. How is this done? By letting your subconscious mind and back muscles govern the shot entirely. You should only be thinking consciously about how well you're aiming at the spot—that's it. Your job now is to sit quietly and wait for things to happen—the plane is flying and you're on autopilot, so to speak.

This method is the most reliable way to shoot a bow, particularly for those who shoot a lot of arrows year after year.

This is how the process works (*this is also discussed in Chapters 7 and 8*).

Using all the proper form tips already discussed, simply draw the bow, get on target and as the sight pin begins to settle on target, just give the shot away! Yes, give it away! You solely focus on the sight pin and target—aiming—and your back muscles will do the rest.

From here, the back muscles will begin their subconscious process to allow the draw-arm elbow and shoulder to pivot rearward. As this happens, tension will build up, the elbow and draw-arm will move imperceptibly rearward, and in a few seconds the shot will go. Either the trigger on your release will break over (even though your finger was never commanded to move) or, if you shoot with a fingers release, your fingers will have gone limp, allowing the bowstring to smoothly slide through your fingers tab or glove.

When done correctly, proper follow-through, with your bow-arm staying up and level with the target as the arrow passes through the bow's riser, will happen naturally. Even if your sight pin wasn't exactly in the bull's-eye when the shot broke, it is amazing how the subconscious and muscle memory work together to execute an accurate shot.

Fact: Releasing the Arrow Should be a Full-Body Experience With the Conscious Mind Focused on One Thing—Aiming at the Target!

Strickland notes that the body and subconscious mind can correct through movement and allow shooting consistency despite what your mind (the conscious one) saw at the moment of the shot. This may sound too good to be true, but any long-time shooter knows it's real. How many times have you shot, with a non-exact aim, and still hit the bull's-eye? A bunch, I would imagine.

Properly training your subconscious mind and back muscles to control the shot will take many weeks, sometimes months, of shot training on a close-range shooting butt. Perform this mostly with your eyes closed to eliminate the interference or distraction of what the conscious mind sees.

No. 10: Follow-Through

To follow through correctly, simply continue looking at the target, with your bow hand up. Allow the bow to vibrate freely until the arrow hits.

Proper follow-through is maintaining focus on the target until the arrow hits. As you do this, it's important to keep the bow elevated just as you did when the arrow left the bow. Keep your hand relaxed, allowing the bow to vibrate and spring naturally (usually out and to the left a bit). Don't drop your bow arm until you hear or see the arrow's impact. That's it.

Don't take any of these techniques lightly. When properly executed, they'll make you the best archery shot you can be.

Chapter 2
The Killer Bow Rig

Stress Forgiveness, Not Speed

"All truths are easy to understand once they are discovered; the point is to discover them."
—Galileo Galilei

A good hunting bow is a forgiving one. When hunting, shots are rarely taken from an ultra-comfortable stand-up position.

I was in an archery shop the other day and watched a customer stroll in looking for a new bow. He shot all the latest and greatest models, but the shop employee pointed out a speed bow that just came in. "This is all the latest technology," he commented. The guy shot the bow a few times at a 15-yard backstop, said, "Wow, this thing's fast and really smooth," and then immediately told the shop rep to wrap it up, all $700 worth.

As I watched the guy shoot, I could tell his shooting form was mediocre at best. Equipped with a critical, non-forgiving speed bow that's really designed for the expert shot, I have no doubt he'll face frustrating days ahead on the range and in the field. The whole spectacle made me cringe.

Fact: Accuracy Kills, Not Speed

Stress Forgiveness

Bowhunting is not 3-D shooting, where you rove a range for targets, relaxingly draw your bow, take methodical aim, and shoot. Nor is it indoor-tournament league, where you stand at 18 meters and punch paper spots all night long in your blue jeans and sandals. Though these archery tasks are absolutely challenging in their own right, they differ from bowhunting.

With bowhunting, the true difficulty lies in the conditions you'll face. They are uncontrollable and almost always unique, because of the weather and terrain, the unpredictability of the animals, the shot angles and shooting positions. Couple all that with the idea of only having "one shot" and the stakes really soar.

Consequently, when it comes to bow accuracy you need all the help you can get. No matter how well you execute the shot in your backyard or on the 3-D range, you'll face shot hiccups in the bowhunting woods. I guarantee it, plain and simple. For this reason, your bow should be *very* forgiving—one that allows for slight errors in shooting form, yet still provides strong shooting accuracy.

It's All in the Specs

Just because a bow shoots smooth and nice on targets does not mean it will function superiorly in the deer woods. Sure a quiet and shock-free bow is nice to have, but its overall geometry will tell you much more about how dependable it will perform at grouping arrows.

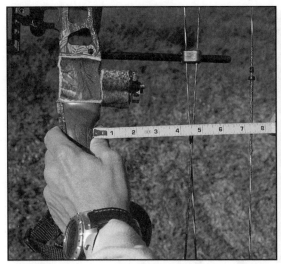 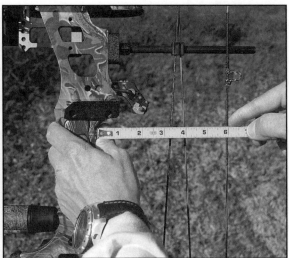

Simply put, the longer the brace height, the more forgiving the bow. However, brace height does affect arrow speed. With a release aid, brace heights around 7 inches allow for a unique blend of speed and forgiveness.

What's a forgiving bow? Though it can get a little tricky, a good gauge to go by is the bow's brace height (probably most important nowadays) and the bow's axle-to-axle length. *I want to explain how a bow's overall geometry, balance, and other variables play a part in how forgiving a bow will shoot as well.*

Brace Height: This measurement from the bow's grip to the bowstring (when it's in the relaxed, un-drawn position) dictates the window of time the arrow stays on the string during the launch process.

The shorter the brace height, the longer the arrow stays on the string. And the longer the arrow stays on the string, the greater the chance for you to disturb it via hand or release torque, or follow-through errors.

The downside to a taller brace height is a shorter power stroke (the distance you draw the bow back from the un-drawn position)—the shorter the power stroke, the slower the arrow speed and the less arrow energy. The key here is to strike up the perfect balance between speed and forgiveness.

A brace height of around 7-to-7 1/2 inches offers a good blend of performance and easy shooting ability for the release-aid shooter. The lines are a little blurry here, too, as short-draw users utilize a shorter power stroke, which shortens the idea of "string time." Theoretically, this means short-draw shooters can get by with slightly shorter brace heights without experiencing loss of forgiveness.

For those using a fingers release, more forgiveness is needed to counter the severe string torque and arrow paradox that occurs once your fingers slip away from the bowstring. In this case, the string is forced to the side, causing intense side-to-side bowstring and arrow movement (paradox), and even possible riser movement. Thus, brace heights of around 8 inches are advised in this case.

 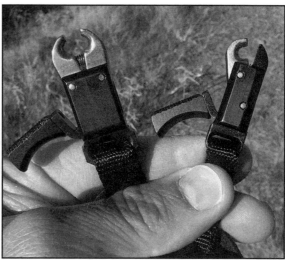

Shorter-axle bows create more string angle at full draw, making it difficult to anchor with the tip of your nose on the bowstring while maintaining a straight, natural head position. A slightly longer draw length and a short-nose release, such as these models by Scott, can solve this problem.

Craig Yehle, an engineer for BowTech, says a longer brace height is more forgiving for at least two reasons. "Since the arrow can't pass through your hand, it must pass some distance above your hand," notes Yehle. "The fact that you are pulling at a point above the grip introduces torque that we refer to as 'vertical torque.' The amount of vertical torque is a function of how far the arrow passes above the hand and the brace height. These two variables define the angle at which you are pulling 'up' on the string—vertical torque. The shorter the brace height, the greater the angle and the greater the vertical torque."

Axle-to-Axle Length: To grasp how a bow's axle length could make it more forgiving, imagine yourself holding two lengths of steel pipe (each at mid-length) and rocking each from side to side. Without a doubt, the longer, heavier length of pipe will be more difficult to move. A longer, and likely heavier, bow will emit the same quality—it'll be harder to torque if hand-twist occurs during the shot, thus making it more accurate to shoot shot after shot.

Yehle explains that a longer bow is more forgiving for at least two reasons: It is generally better to place the peep closer to the eye, which is accomplished with less string angle (accomplished with longer axle-to-axle length). And a bow with a higher moment of inertia with respect to the grip will be more stable (back to the steel pipe analogy). Generally speaking, the longer the bow, the higher the moment of inertia, especially if the riser is longer. "The addition of weight at the ends of the riser is a good method for increasing this effect," maintains Yehle.

"Theoretically, a longer bow should be less susceptible to high and low misses and a longer brace height bow should be less susceptible to high, low, left and right misses," he adds.

Fact: Longer Bows Help Minimize High and Low Misses

Ideal Release Bow

The author's good friend, Jim Velazquez, insists on using a quiet, accurate, and fast set-up for hunting.

Most of today's bowhunters use a release aid to shoot a bow. Unquestionably this is the most accurate way to shoot a bow. With a small metal jaw clipping to the bowstring, or string loop, to free the bowstring is very precise and crisp and nearly torque free compared to holding the bowstring directly with fingers. Fingers tend to quiver all over the place and make pressure distribution more complicated.

Also, because of its low torque, a release aid allows near-straight arrow flight at take-off—another accuracy advantage. A release aid also allows the use of a faster and more compact bow. Bows with axle lengths ranging from 30-to-38 inches are ideal for release-aid shooting. However, keep in mind that some of these bows are not the best designs for serious bowhunting. Key points to look for in a forgiving, easy-to-shoot, and moderately fast hunting bow include:

Draw Cycle & Letoff: For serious hunting, choose a bow with a smooth, nearly strain-free draw cycle. Savvy bow engineers are placing high value on cam systems that draw smoothly but remain uniquely fast. This is great news. In the past, if you wanted fast, you had to put up with harsh, bumpy draw cycles—a true liability in the field, particularly in slow-drawing situations. A harsh draw cycle, one that builds up drawing force quickly and awkwardly during the initial draw and stays harsh almost the entire length of the cycle, also tends to "flex" your drawing muscles to a point where it's harder to relax them once you reach full draw and begin to aim.

Bows like the Mathews Switchback XT, Hoyt Vectrix Plus, and Bow Tech Guardian, to name a few, all boast smooth draws, yet deliver great arrow power and speed.

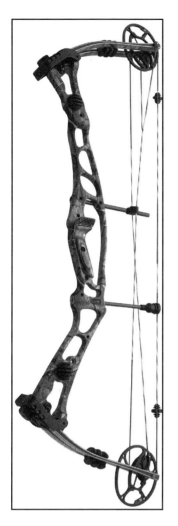
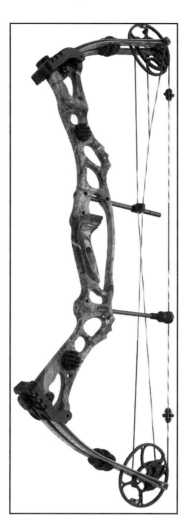
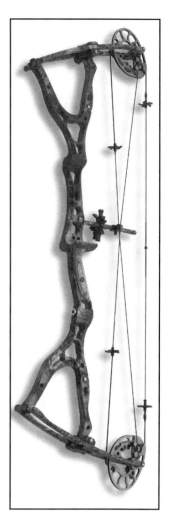
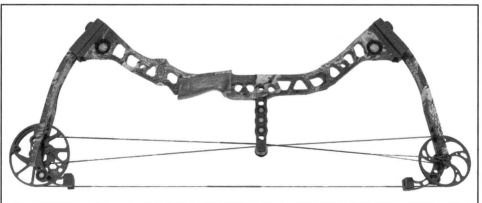

Clockwise from left: Hoyt's Katera XL and Vectrix Plus, Bow Tech's Guardian, and Mathews Switchback XT are great examples of smooth, fast and forgiving hunting bows.

Bows with smooth-drawing cams and gentle letoff valleys are ideal for serious bowhunting. They are user friendy in the deer woods.

Most bowhunters favor a high letoff valley since it's easier to hold for prolonged periods at full draw. Many archers claim improved "aiming" with high letoff as well. For this reason, the majority of today's bows have 70-to-80-percent letoff cam systems. However, the downsides to high letoff are slightly slower arrow speeds, and greater string torque at release (when a flaw occurs), since there's less pressure on the release-aid jaws during initial takeoff.

I tend to favor letoffs in the 65-to-75 percent range. But I will say this; don't ever sacrifice an ultra-short valley for low letoff. These types of bows can be distracting to shoot well in fast-shooting, "heated" bowhunting situations. In this case, I'd opt for a slightly higher letoff from the standpoint of pure shooting comfort.

Brace Height: Generally speaking, bows with brace heights below 7 inches don't make versatile hunting companions. If you have a somewhat short draw length (26-to-about 27 ½ inches) the minimum brace height for you could be closer to 6 ¾ inches.

Notes on Speed: Speed bows typically have IBO-rated speeds of 330 fps and higher, and come with "performance"-minded brace heights between 5 ¾-to-6 ¼ inches. Such bows can make any flaw in your shooting form detrimental to accuracy. This is why I don't recommend them for serious bowhunting conditions where awkward shooting positions are more the rule than the exception. IBO-rated bows in the 305-to-320 fps range are easier to shoot yet still provide flat, powerful arrow trajectory.

Shoot Fingers?

The number of compound shooters using a fingers release could be dwindling, but many veteran, long-time shooters favor this technique for perhaps four specific reasons: simplicity, higher challenge, shooting speed (very fast and fluid), and for the intimate, spiritual feel it provides. Though not as accurate as using a mechanical release aid, a well-practiced and

BY JOE BELL

Don't ever sacrifice pinpoint accuracy for speed. The author shot this gray fox using an ultra-accurate fingers set-up—a Mathews Apex bow, which measures 42-¼ inches axle to axle, and utilizes an 8-inch brace height.

well-conditioned fingers shooter can release with surprising accuracy. The trick to achieving such consistency starts with choosing the proper bow.

Bow Length: With fingers, always choose a longer bow. Shorter bows offer acute string angles at full draw, which can place vertical pressure on fingers and make a smooth, gentle release nearly impossible. Also, the sharper the string angle, the better the release must be. If you fail to keep the back of your hand vertical through the release, excessive horizontal string oscillation will result, complicating tuning, broadhead flight and accuracy.

Proper bow length for fingers shooting varies depending on your draw length. I'm a long-time fingers shooter. With a 28-inch draw length, I tend to favor bows in the 41-to-44-inch range. Keep in mind, a bow's brace height and cam design/size also affect a bow's string angle at full draw, so these are general guidelines. I highly recommend shooting bows in a pro shop to see which ones provide comfortable, accurate shooting. *(Note:* Pay close attention to how the bowstring comes off the eccentrics at full draw; some are positioned high on the eccentrics, which result in less sting angle.) Those with longer draw lengths of 29 inches or more may favor slightly longer designs. And vice versa with shorter draw lengths.

The manner in which you grip the string also affects bow length. Some fingers shooters use only two fingers (or 1 ½) to release the bowstring. In this case, slightly shorter bows (37-to-39 inches axle to axle) provide the necessary shooting comfort.

I favor a split-finger grip where I place my index finger above the nock, and my two longer fingers below. At full draw, I drop most of the weight off the top and bottom fingers. With this type of method, I can draw and release the fastest yet with excellent accuracy. Also, I can "control" the arrow better in the case of an arrow pop off.

After more than a decade of experimenting, I continue to favor bows with full-draw string angles of around 47-to-45 degrees (with my 28-inch draw) or less. Two of my favorite fingers bows at this time are the Mathews' Apex and Hoyt Montega.

Though I can shoot shorter string angles just fine, in uncontrolled bowhunting situations I want a smoother, longer and more-forgiving rig.

Brace Height: For years I shot a Mathews Conquest III with MiniMax cams with exceptional accuracy. However, in some highly emotional bowhunting situations, I found when I "rough" released, this bow was not the most-forgiving bow, because of its 6 ¾-to 7-inch brace height. For this reason, I favor bows with at least a 7 ½-inch brace height, with 8-inches or more being ideal. The above bows I just mentioned offer this trait.

Cam Geometry: This is a biggie to me. With fingers, I prefer a smoother draw cycle when compared to a release-aid bow, mainly because I'm holding the bow's drawing weight entirely with the ends of my fingers and not a mechanical tool that's fastened to my wrist or gripped heavily in my hand.

A smooth draw cycle-to-valley transition is even more important for the fingers shooter. With fingers, we tend to creep a bit when settling in or when holding for extended

---

TECH TIPS

Parallel-Limb Bows: Designed for Accuracy?

Today's bows are beginning to look like half-shaped boxes with almost abrupt 90-degree angled limbs. Mathews discovered years ago that limbs nearly parallel to each other shoot much more quietly and with less vibration, since each limb is working in equal and opposite directions.

However, in the last couple years, bow engineers have continued to take this limb geometry to the extreme. In some cases, bows now come with "beyond parallel" limb design.

Are there any accuracy downsides to this radical design? Some experts say yes, some say no.

"I think today's short, parallel-limb bows are just as accurate as more traditional-length compound bows," says Darin Cooper, senior product engineer for Hoyt USA. "However, most target shooters still prefer bows with more traditional-limb angles, because they provide the archer with more feedback on their shots through recoil."

David Kronengold, vice president of engineering for Precision Shooting Equipment, told me a bow's axle length has more to do with physical comfort and less to do with accuracy, assuming you use a nock loop. He believes short bows are every bit as accurate as longer models. "I have seen pro shooters Chance Beauboef, Nathan Brooks and Eric Griggs shoot amazing rounds with our hunting-geometry bows. They prefer longer bows, but they are just as accurate with the shorter ones," he says.

To fully understand this, realize that today's short bows are built much differently. With swept-back limb geometry, they have longer, heavier risers to boost axle-to-axle length. This type of riser geometry actually increases holding and aiming stability, which makes them shoot very well by countering any loss of axle length.

Cooper says, "These bows actually feel longer, because there's more mass at the ends of the bow to resist canting. Really, your form, string angle and intended usage should still be considered when determining your optimum bow length."

However, Craig Yehle, director of research & development for BowTech, has another opinion. "I think longer risers are more forgiving, and I think parallel limbs are slightly less forgiving," he said. "Parallel limbs do some great things (increase efficiency, reduce shock, reduce shot noise, etc.). But I believe there is some tradeoff in forgiveness. A bow with less limb angle will have a greater rearward thrust at the shot (hand shock). If a rearward thrust originates at the cams and forces the bow back into the shooter's hand, the bow is inherently stabilized against left and right (horizontal) torque at the shot. The absence of this thrust reduces this potential benefit, nevertheless, the market wants absolute minimal hand shock, so we offer this with many of our bows."

periods of time. For serious bowhunting, I avoid bows that rudely jerk you back into the raw force of the draw when you creep just a tad. I say save these for the 3-D course.

In most cases, a smoother draw means less arrow energy, but I'm willing to sacrifice this for shooting comfort, which is the most important attribute in a true hunting bow. Perhaps more important is the type of draw valley and "wall" the cam system provides.

I use a dynamic release to free the bowstring, so I prefer cams that offer a solid stop or wall at full draw. This way, I can relax and pull up against this wall as I apply back-tension during the aiming process.

However, some fingers shooters have a "dead" release, where they acquire the right aim and simply relax their fingers to release the arrow.

Both release styles will require different cam geometry. A dynamic release goes best with a hard wall. A stagnant-type fingers release is more complemented by a longer, more "mushy" full-draw valley, because of the sometimes slight "creeping" that can occur with this release method. With a longer valley, draw-length imperfections are well tolerated and top accuracy is still achieved.

For the dynamic fingers release (one uses back tension as part of the let-go process; see chapter 8 for more information on this), I'd recommend draw letoffs no higher than 65 percent. For the "dead" release fingers shooter (where only the "relaxing" of the hand and fingers lets the string go), 65 or 60 percent and lower are preferred so more back-tension is acquired at full draw, resulting in improved accuracy.

You can add various types of counterweights or dampening systems to make your hunting bow quieter and better balanced. Sims' Mini Extreme Limbsaver System attaches to the bow's limb bolts. This accessory not only hushes bow noise but also adds weight at the outer ends of the bow's riser, which increases shooting stability.

Chuck Adams, a staunch fingers shooter, uses a dead-style release. He draws, anchors hard against his face, and then creeps a ½-inch before settling into his anchor. From here, he comes up to target, holds for a split second and releases by relaxing the back of his hand. Shooting this way, his accuracy is best using a 50-percent letoff.

"To aim is not enough, you must hit!"
—German Proverb

Minimizing Bow Torque

Bow Design: As stated earlier, a longer, heavier bow is harder to torque. However, most bowhunters favor a more compact bow for optimum maneuverability in the woods, especially when hunting from a tree stand or ground blind. In this case, do what you can to make your short bow as torque resistant as possible.

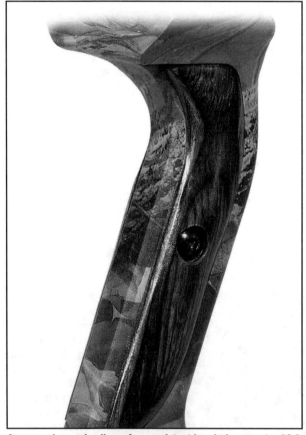

A narrow bow grip allows for consistent hand placement, which minimizes hand torque.

Today's bow market is flooded with compact, parallel-style limb bows that use an extra-long riser. Though these types of bows are short, they emit the feel of a longer, more stable bow since the riser weight is spread out over a longer vertical plane. This increases stability two-fold.

Another trick to increasing bow stability is to strategically add counterweights at the far ends of the bow's riser. Mathews, a very innovative bow company, places vibration dampers at the ends of all its bow risers. These not only make the bow quieter to shoot and with less recoil, but these weights (which come in various weights, including aluminum, brass or ultra-heavy tungsten versions) increase the vertical inertia of the bow, making it more "sway" or torque resistant.

Another trick I've found is to attach Sims Laboratories' Mini Extreme Limbsaver System to a bow. These 3-ounce donut-shaped vibration dampers are truly effective at cutting down on shot noise, but they also place a bit more weight at the ends of the bow riser, which increases stability. You can increase their weight by adding counterweights to the dampers' outside threaded portions.

Bow Grip: If you used a bow to drive with, then the grip would have to be its steering wheel. This is the critical contact area that helps you control the bow during the shot. If you grip the bow wrong, torque will occur and it'll show on the shot.

The author recommends using the Shrewd grip with many bows, since it offers a narrow throat and base, ensuring better accuracy.

To counter bow-hand torque, choose a comfortable yet somewhat narrow grip. A narrow grip offers one important thing: with less surface area, it minimizes the chance you'll grip it differently from shot to shot.

As was illustrated in Chapter 1, the pressure point of the bow should lie somewhere near the base of your thumb. This point of contact is the most stable, and with a narrow grip, it'll be easier to place the point of the grip in this exact spot. With a wider grip, this pressure point area is easy to overlap, making it a bit more tedious to place your hand exactly in the same spot.

With most of my bows today, I remove the wood panel and shoot directly off the riser's self-grip. Although this type of bow grip may feel awkward at first, you'll likely appreciate its consistency in just a short time.

Randy Ulmer told me he hasn't used a screw-on grip for 15 years, and insists on gripping the riser part for the narrowest, most torque-free grip possible.

Of course, if you often hunt in cold weather, an all-wood grip or a "riser" grip wrapped with a layer or two of hockey tape to warm it will provide more shooting comfort. And in this case, I'd be willing to give up a little bit of consistency for shooting comfort, as long as my hunting didn't require pinpoint accuracy (such as close-range tree-stand shots). Keep in mind, Hoyt, BowTech, and other companies offer great one-piece wood grips that are still narrow and torque resistant.

You can also add tape or fleece to all portions of the grip except for the back or "pressure point" of the grip. This will allow the palm of your hand to slide into position, consistently.

Another option is to upgrade your current wood grip with a custom offering. Shrewd, Hicks, Loesch, and Torque Less make excellent custom grips that enhance the qualities you need to shoot as torque free as possible, such as a narrow base and throat. For example, I prefer to shoot a Shrewd all-aluminum grip on my Mathews bows that come with wood grips.

Fact: Narrow Bow Grips Ensure Consistent Hand Placement, Improving Accuracy

A bow sling allows you to relax your bow hand without fear of dropping the bow. This creates better accuracy for some archers. The author recommends a fleece sling, which is quiet and comfortable to use in the woods. Also, a rear-mounted stabilizer such as the Doinker Chubby Hunter, is an important accessory for properly balancing a bow, particularly one that tends to tip forward excessively.

Even with the pressure point of the bow well centralized in your hand, you still need to keep a totally relaxed hand and arm during the shot. Thus, keep your fingers limp and loosely wrapped around the grip. The fingers are the messengers for the rest of the hand and bow arm. Tight, grip-clenching fingers will likely twist the bow handle at the shot, creating torque. Conversely, consistency is created since relaxed fingers don't disturb the bow during arrow delivery.

When using a relaxed hand on the grip, you'll often find it impossible to harness the bow during the shot; it will inadvertently fall from your hand! To prevent this, use a bow sling.

I often tuck three of my bow-hand fingers along the side of the grip and use my index finger to loosely grasp the bow. However, you should experiment with positioning your fingers in the most comfortable and relaxed manner.

Bow Balance & Stabilizers

A shock-absorbing stabilizer not only dulls shot sound, but also creates a steadier aim. This is the 6-inch model offered by Fuse.

Most bowhunters overlook bow balance, but bows that don't tip back or too much forward when held out in front of you, when un-drawn, tend to shoot and aim better compared to awkwardly balanced bows.

Some bows balance better than others right out of the box. To offset those that don't, use counterweights to make these bows hold plumb. Bows with reflexed-type risers tend to tip downward, even without a front-mounted stabilizer. To correct this, you'll have to add a short counterweight somewhere below the grip on the bowstring-side of the bow. Doinker's Chubby Hunter provides the perfect accessory.

I often add front and back riser weight until my bow balances the way I like it. I like to use a fairly long front stabilizer, so my bow not only aims more steadily, but also functions with more torque resistance.

Your hunting bow is basically your partner in crime when you head for the woods. Choose one that's quiet and reliable and simply gets the job done, no matter the situation, rather than one that's flashy, kind of loud, fast shooting and usually full of empty promises. You get the picture.

BY JOE BELL

Chapter 3
The 10-Step Bow Tune-Up

Achieving Perfect Arrow Flight

"Knowledge becomes power only when we put it into use."
—Anonymous

Precise arrow tuning creates a more forgiving, accurate set-up. This three-arrow group was shot from 55 yards.

Don't you hate the guy that shows up in bowhunting camp and relentlessly drills the target's bull's-eye out to 50-plus yards? Yes, you hate him but at the same time you feel a little bit envious of him. Certainly, this kind of bowhunter is highly skilled. But his bow set-up also has a lot to do with his performance.

This is where a well-refined, tuned bow comes into play. It offers increased performance in every way, since it's quieter, more accurate and extremely forgiving of shooting errors—everything you need to boost your shooting confidence and look good in front of a crowd.

Straight, true arrow flight lies at the foundation of a well-tuned bow. However, this trait doesn't happen naturally and is only possible when certain prerequisites are met: By using a well-conditioned, functional bow; properly spined arrow shafts; a quality arrow rest; and finally, performing precise bow/arrow tuning techniques.

I recommend each of these specific set-up tips to complete your tuning process. *Note:* Before beginning this phase, be sure your bow is fully outfitted with all the accessories you plan on hunting with (peep sight, string silencers, stabilizer, bow quiver, etc.); any changes in your set-up could affect the bow's overall tune.

Step No. 1
Inspect Cam Rollover & Wheel Lean

Before straight arrow flight can happen, your bow must function perfectly. The most important aspect of this pertains to the bow's eccentrics—they must work in harmony. In other words, if the bow's cams don't rollover in total unison, placing each buss cable into the cam's string tracks simultaneously, then the energy transferred to the arrow isn't centralized, since the bowstring will cycle the arrow's nock up and down. This badly disrupts arrow flight and hurts arrow speed.

The first thing I do with a new bow is grasp the bowstring and draw it back. However, I slow the draw down just before reaching the cam's valley. If the bow is a hybrid or 1 ½ cam system, I glance down at the bottom or power cam and verify how the cable is hitting the draw stop. At the same time, I also visually check the control cam above and see how the cable is bisecting the stop—if there is one. Optimally, the cables will hit the draw stops at exactly the same time. This applies to both a hybrid and two-cam system. You can adjust cable length until the cable wrap is identical, allowing for synchronized rollover.

To know what you're looking for, you will need to reference the bow's owner's manual; the manufacturer's Web site; call the company's support desk; or ask a qualified pro shop for assistance.

With single-cam bows, cam rollover is a non-issue since there's only one cam on the system. However, be sure the bottom/power cam is orientated in the optimum position. This allows for top performance, and most importantly, level nock travel throughout the draw cycle.

Again, reference the bow's owner's manual, go to the manufacturer's Web site or contact it by phone.

Also, some bows come with split-yoke cable harnesses at either one or both ends, and some don't have any. Those that do allow you to alter cam or wheel lean. Ideally, you want zero to very little lean in the full-draw position.

The split-yoke basically takes up the limb's load at full draw and is designed to equalize the pressure on each side of the limb. Simply twist one side of the split-yoke to balance out the load, which corrects cam lean. You'll need a bow press for this. Some cam lean is okay in those cases where the bow doesn't have a split yoke in place, but too much lean can lead to poor arrow-nock travel and accuracy.

Step No. 2
Set Bow's Tiller

This is a simple process. With a two-cam or hybrid-cam bow, adjust the limbs for even tiller. This means the distance from the bowstring to the limb base will be the same. Use a ruler or arrow to verify this setting and loosen or tighten limb bolts until even tiller is achieved.

With a single-cam bow, it's best to simply crank down on the limb bolts until they stop, and then back them out in equal rotations until you reach proper pull weight. That's it.

Fact: Bowstrings must stabilize/creep before precise arrow tuning can be achieved. This means shooting the bow for a hundred shots or so, then beginning the tuning process.

Step No. 3
Draw Length and Draw Weight

Using all the tips in Chapter 2, make sure your bow's draw length is set perfectly. (Also, do all you can to get the bow's draw weight set where you want it during this phase.) If not, you could alter the adjustment of your drop-away rest. Because a drop-away rest uses a nylon cord that attaches to the bow's downward-moving cable, and pulls the arrow arm up as the bow is being drawn, any alteration in the draw length could affect how fast or slow the arrow arm raises, which could affect the bow's tune.

1.

2.

3.

4.

Before tuning, be sure to set your draw weight accordingly. For hunting, proper draw weight means a smooth pull from any position, such as this one.

There are a couple ways to alter draw length besides making adjustments to the bow's cams. For very small adjustment, you can twist up the bowstring (to shorten draw) or untwist it (to lengthen draw).

If you don't want to alter the bowstring length (because of peep alignment), you can also twist or untwist the buss cables to achieve a similar result. In this case, however, twisting up the string means a slight increase in draw length, and untwisting means a reduction. When doing this, be sure to consult your bow's owner's manual to be sure you maintain correct rotation of the cam(s) for peak efficiency and proper cycling of the arrow.

Note: When altering buss cable length, be sure to add an equal number of twists or untwists to each opposing string on a hybrid or two-cam system so that cam synchronization remains unaltered.

Personally, I usually shoot my bows at their maximum peak weight. In some cases, I'll add several more additional twists to the cables/harnesses, which increases peak weight and brace height a smidge, and slightly preloads the limbs for quieter shooting. In some cases, the bow's draw valley becomes firmer by doing this, which creates a more accurate, positive stop.

Note: Be careful not to exceed the bow's advertised peak weight by more than a couple of pounds, or you could void the bow's warranty.

Step No. 4
Arrow Rest Set-Up

Using a Release-Aid: Even with a smooth release and proper arrow spine, an arrow cycling through the bow still oscillates. To ensure a consistent launch and accurate, clean arrow flight, the arrow rest must do what it can to stabilize the shaft during those initial inches of forward arrow travel, yet allow unimpeded fletching clearance as the rear portion of the arrow clears the rest.

This is one reason why a drop-away rest remains the optimum choice. At the shot, the holding arm is up to initially support the arrow during the first portion of arrow takeoff, then simply drops out of the way so the arrow and its vanes can pass totally unencumbered without the chance of shaft or vane contacting the arm.

Also, if the archer slightly torques the bow handle during the shot, a drop-away minimizes this error since the arrow falls downward and has no contact with the arrow. The result? Maximum forgiveness and perfect arrow flight, given the arrow spine is correct and the release is smooth.

Another important feature to the drop-away rest is fast-loading capability. Simply snap the arrow on the string and lay the arrow on the arrow trough mounted on the bow's shelf. There's no gentle seating involved between a split-prong launching arm; you can just load and go.

Of course, some drop-away rests are poorly designed and cause contact with the arrow. Over the years I've tried a lot of great models and I can recommend these models wholeheartedly: Trophy Taker Extreme FC, AAE/Cavalier Avalanche, Quality Archery Designs Ultra-Rest, New Archery Products Smart Rest, and Trophy Ridge Drop Zone.

To optimize performance, adjust your rest so the arrow holding arm stays up as long as possible without causing collision with the arrow's fletching. This process can be tricky and tedious, which is certainly the downside to the drop rest. In some cases, it may be impossible to use a drop-away if your bow cycles arrows erratically up and down. Here, you're better off with a traditional launcher or full-containment rest that allows more cushioning of the arrow during arrow launch.

1.

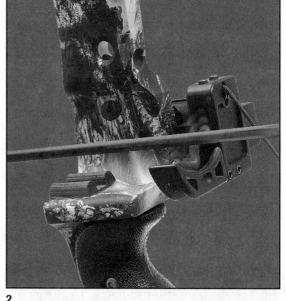

2.

When set up properly, a drop-away rest supports the arrow initially, but then the holding arm falls down just in time for the fletching to clear. This is the Trophy Ridge Drop Zone in action.

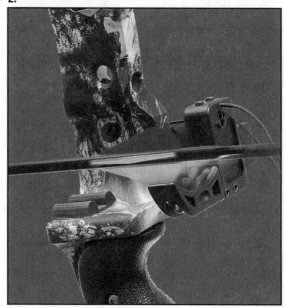

3.

Using a Fingers Release: The old-fashioned fingers release causes unavoidable side-to-side movement at arrow takeoff. This requires a special arrow rest, one that "cushions" or dampens this horizontal arrow travel.

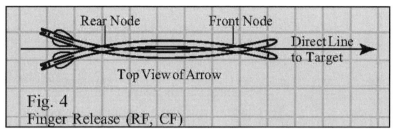

Fig. 4
Finger Release (RF, CF)

Once an arrow is released with fingers, the arrow undergos a series of small bends, which is a process known as paradox. The arrow will take two-to-three slight bends before clearing the rest. At the release, the center of the shaft curves very slightly inward toward the bow riser, then more pronounced outward, and then back inward as it clears the rest. Arrow spine has a large affect on how the arrow oscillates. Arrow oscillation also occurs with arrows shot with a mechanical release. Only this paradox is usually not as intense, depending on arrow spine.

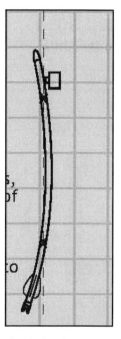

The tried-and-true flipper/plunger combination rest is tops. Great models include the AAE Cavalier Free Flyte, Terry Deluxe, or Cartel flipper rest, used in tandem with a quality screw-in cushion plunger such as the Cavalier Master-Lok plunger.

Many pro-level fingers shooters use the Bodoodle rest as well since it has two flexible steel blades, each providing lateral and horizontal stability for optimum control using a fingers release.

My favorite arrow-rest set-up is custom made. I use an old-style stick-on New Archery Flipper II rest, which is affixed to a thin aluminum plate that I glue on using contact cement to the bow's riser or overdraw attachment. This gives the rest's flipper arm enough horizontal extension to accommodate modern bow risers. I use a Cavalier Master-Lok plunger with this set-up. This system creates the utmost reliability and quiet performance I demand in a super-accurate hunting rest. I've used this kind of rest in the toughest hunting conditions without a lick of failure. However, I'm also quite fond of the Cavalier Free Flyte rest as well.

Another choice is the new Trophy Ridge Drop Zone Free-style drop-away rest. I've only tested this rest a few times and it appears accurate. However, some experts believe a standard non-drop arrow rest is more beneficial with fingers shooting since it offers more arrow stability throughout arrow transfer, resulting in better consistency overall.

Fact: Unimpeded fletching clearance is a prerequisite of precise arrow tuning.

Step No. 5
Center Shot

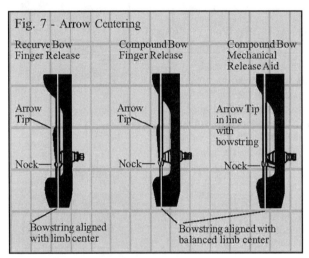

Fig. 7 - Arrow Centering

Recurve Bow
Finger Release

Compound Bow
Finger Release

Compound Bow
Mechanical
Release Aid

Arrow
Tip

Arrow
Tip

Arrow Tip
in line
with
bowstring

Nock

Nock

Nock

Bowstring aligned
with limb center

Bowstring aligned with
balanced limb center

Proper center shot means the bowstring and arrow rest are perfectly in line with one another so the energy is centralized to the arrow. With a release-aid, the arrow should be perfectly centered with the bowstring and the grooves in the cams. With a fingers release, place the tip of the arrow slightly off center, to the left 1/16-to-1/8-inch for a right-handed shooter.

A center-shot alignment tool such as the Archery BowPlane by Double Take Archery makes proper set-up a snap. This tool projects a visible laser line that you can line up with the cams, bow grip and arrow rest. This eliminates eyeballing center-shot position.

Center shot is the position of the arrow rest and arrow in relation to the bow's bowstring. For top performance, accuracy, and easy tunability, the arrow must be positioned in-line with the bowstring's natural forward path of movement, which will direct all power into the arrow nock and not to one side or the other.

A lot of archers today rely on laser-alignment tools to do this, which is a good idea. However, I've set center shot for years with nothing else but my plain old eyes. The technique I use is to place the arrow on the bowstring and center it on the arrow arm. Then I hold the bow out at arm's length, resting the bottom cam on my knee. From here, I glance up and down at the bottom and top cams, and do my best to center the bowstring in each of the cam's string groove where the bowstring wraps around at full draw.

With some bows, you'll notice the bowstring doesn't run inline with each string groove at the same time. In this case, I visually center the bowstring in the bottom cam's string groove and adjust the arrow rest so the arrow is visually centered with the center of the bowstring. That's a perfect center shot for a release-aid set-up.

Do the same thing when shooting fingers, but you will want the arrow's point slightly to the left (1/16-to-1/8-inch to the left for a right-handed shooter). This corrects for the fingers' horizontal push-off of the arrow once the bowstring is freed. This allows for the best tune possible, since the bowstring doesn't travel in its natural forward-moving path as the string slips out of nimble, multiple fingers.

Step No. 6
Adjust Arrow Rest

Release-Aid/Drop-Away Rest: Begin by adjusting the holding arm so that it pops up a couple of inches before you reach full-draw. This will allow the arm to stabilize the arrow initially during arrow takeoff, but still fall in time for the arrow's fletching to clear. Using small vanes, such as the 2-inch AAE Max Hunter or 2-inch Bohning Blazer, will make tuning easier with a drop-away, because the distance between the point of the arrow and the front end of the fletching is extended. This increases the time in which the arrow-holding arm has to stay up and to support the arrow better, before it must drop down to get out of the way.

TECH TIPS

Note: Bow's Final Tune/Set-Up

Once your bow is delivering arrows straight and true, record every possible specification on the bow, including brace height, axle-to-axle length, draw weight, tiller height, nock height, limb-bolt position, arrow rest location (vertically and horizontally), draw length (measure using an arrow and note exact center of where arrow bisects arrow-rest hole), etc.

Once the tuning process is complete, also record the arrow's speed and draw out the exact type of paper tear achieved. Then place all this information in a notepad and a 3 x 5 index card. The index card should ride in your bow's case at all times.

Some archers prefer to keep the arm up as long as possible to prevent any inconsistencies in the case of a bow's poor nock travel, or to simply stabilize the arrow better during the launching process. This is good, but fletching can collide with the holding arm as a result. Also, one of the perceived advantages of using a drop-away rest is to reduce potential torque during the shot between the arrow and rest. To maximize this, you want to get that launcher arm down as quickly as possible.

Clearance Issues: In some cases, fletching contact will occur with drop-aways regardless of arrow-arm travel. A good remedy is to try increasing the spring tension of the holding arm. Nearly all quality drop-aways allow for some spring-tension adjustability. With fast arrows, increase the tension to maximum.

Also, you can align arrow fletching to enhance clearance even more. With many rests, I've had the best luck shooting the arrow cock-vane up (off color vane up). Simply experiment and see what works best for you.

Nock height: Adjust the nock height so it's about 1/8-inch above center.

Fingers Release/Flipper-Plunger Rest: The position of the flipper is important for optimum arrow clearance and tuning. Adjust it so that it supports the arrow, laterally, just enough and no more. In other words, position the arm so it doesn't extend beyond the arrow's shaft (a little beyond the shaft is okay, however). This allows for the very best arrow, fletching and nock clearance as the arrow swings from side to side (known as arrow paradox) at release, passes the rest, and leaves the bow. A good flipper arm folds down at the very slightest touch, so some arrow/vane contact is totally acceptable.

Initial plunger tension varies depending on the bow type, brace height and arrow spine. According to Dick Tone, director of archery for AAE/Cavalier, stiffer plunger tension usually goes best with recurve bows and softer tension for compounds. A recurve's lack of letoff delivers more thrust to the arrow at takeoff, requiring more plunger tension to control the arrow.

This is a good fingers tear in paper from about 6 feet away. Note the horizontal tear is about ¾-inch wide, with evidence of the tip near the middle.

With my compound set-ups, I've found the plunger's "light" spring usually yields more forgiving broadhead flight. However, I suggest you begin your tuning with the "medium" spring (usually 2 or 3 spring types are included with the Cavalier plunger) just to be safe and adjust the plunger button to a pretty soft setting.

To do this, back out the small spring screw as much as possible, while making sure that once the plunger is compressed, it pops back up to its full outward extension on its own. Too light of a setting usually causes the plunger to "sag" and not reach its full outward position. This is a good initial set-up in which to begin the tuning process.

Nock height: Adjust the nock height so it's about 3/8-inch above center.

Step No. 7
Record Bow Set-Up, "Shoot In" Bowstrings & Adjust Peep Height

At this point, it's a good idea to make a few "set-up" marks using a non-permanent felt pen. Draw a line on each bow's cam, noting how it bisects the limb. Also, measure the brace height (distance from bowstring to bow grip's throat) and axle-to-axle length of the bow. Measure the tiller height on each limb as well.

Next, begin shooting the bow at close range. Do this for at least 100-to-200 shots, or more. This will allow the strings to creep slightly/settle in if you have made any twists to the bowstring or if the bowstrings are brand-new. The newer the bowstrings, the more you should shoot them in. There's no reason to start tuning if the length of the bow's strings will change, as this tends to alter cam synchronization, peak weight, draw length, nock height, etc.

> **TECH TIPS**
>
> ### Notes on Nock-to-Bowstring Fit
>
> There are a lot of suggestions out there regarding proper nock fit, but I prefer my nocks to snap on with some security and be able to slide up and down the string but with a light amount of pressure. Perhaps the best way to determine good nock fit is to snap the arrow on and then grasp the arrow shaft and wiggle it from side to side. The nock should only "rock" very slightly. Too much side-to-side deviation will affect accuracy.
>
> To get nock fit just right, you may have to remove and apply new center serving on the bowstring, or be sure to tell your custom string maker the exact type of arrow nock you use.

Once you've made all your marks and completed the shots, reverify the bow's set-up marks and readjust as needed. If adjustments are required, twist up strings/harnesses, and readjust peak weight until everything meets initial set-up specs. Then shoot the bow again for several more shots. Do this until everything stays consistent, despite shooting, and then you're ready for the next step.

It's always a good idea to shoot your bow for a bit to allow any initial string creep to occur, and then conduct final tuning.

Peep Adjustment: Now is also the right time to readjust your peep sight so that it's at proper height and alignment.

Step No. 8
Bare-Shaft Tune

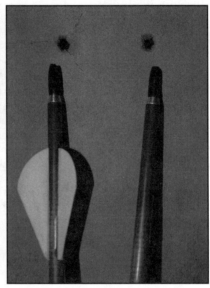

Shooting through paper from 6 feet away is a sure-fire way of correcting wobbly arrow flight. With a release-aid, a clean "bullet hole" tear indicates perfect arrow flight.

Now is the time to check for proper arrow flight. Initially, the best way to do this is with a standard arrow but with no fletching. To duplicate the weight of the fletching, add a few inches or so of electrician's tape. This method was invented by Chuck Adams and is called the Weight Compensation Tuning Method. Next, shoot it through taut paper from about 6 feet away. With a release-aid, the goal is a near perfect "bullet hole," about the size of the arrow shaft itself. With a fingers release, it's best to take a non-permanent felt pen and dab the front of the arrow's tip. Then shoot it into paper. The ideal fingers tear is a slight horizontal rip, about ¾-inch wide, with the tip's marker smear near the middle of the tear, or more to the left, identifying a slightly "stiff" arrow rather than a weak one (for the right-handed shooter).

In the accompanying sidebar, you'll find a trouble-shooting section on correcting arrow flight problems. Another excellent source for paper tuning is Easton's *Maintenance and Tuning Guide*. The complete guide is now available online at **www.eastonarchery.com**. Just click on the "downloads" tab.

Easton's *Tuning and Maintenance Guide* is a great source on bow tuning.

Fixing Arrow Flight

When paper tuning, make the following adjustments to your arrow rest and/or nockpoint height to remedy any vertical or horizontal arrow movement. Also, be sure to make only very slight adjustments at a time until the problem is eliminated. Also, correct vertical movements first, then proceed to horizontal correction.

Finally, in some cases, you might have a poor tear that continues no matter what you do. In this case, I strongly urge you to paper tune with a stiffer-spine arrow, like the next arrow size up. A very weak arrow can come out of a bow like a noodle, causing various tears and inconsistencies. A stiffer arrow usually remedies the problem.

High Vertical Tear (CR and CF): This tear indicates a high nockpoint height. To correct high tear, lower nockpoint 1/16-inch at a time until the problem is eliminated. If this doesn't do it, double check vane clearance, and if the clearance looks good, try a stiffer arrow shaft (with release-aid).

Keep in mind that a high tear could mean a number of other things, too, such as the bow's nock travel is not level, arrow rest launcher arm is too stiff, spring tension on drop-away arm is too stiff or is dropping incorrectly, or the bow could have dry or damaged wheel axles.

Continue to make adjustments to your arrow rest (spring tension and arrow-holding arm travel) until the tear is eliminated. If problem persists, have a pro-shop tech inspect the bow's nock travel and cam bushings and axles.

Low Vertical Tear (CR and CF): To correct, raise nockpoint 1/16-inch at a time until the problem is corrected. Also, increase spring tension on the rest.

Right Horizontal Tear (CR): This is a common tear for right-handed release-aid shooters. Generally indicates that arrow rest position is too far to the right, or there is possible vane contact on inside of arrow launcher arm. To correct, move arrow rest to left in small increments. If this problem persists, then you may need to try a different arrow rest that allows for increased horizontal movement.

For CF and RF, this tear indicates a stiff arrow reaction. To correct, increase bow weight, use a slightly heavier point, decrease side-rest pressure, or use a weaker-spine arrow. For left-handed shooters, perform the opposite.

Left Horizontal Tear (CR): This usually indicates a weak-arrow reaction and/or clearance problems. To correct, move arrow rest to the right in small increments until problem is eliminated, or decrease bow weight, or choose a stiffer-spine arrow. For CF and RF, this tear indicates a weak arrow reaction. To correct, choose a stiffer arrow, or increase side-rest pressure, or decrease bow weight. You may also want to check for clearance issues. Left-handed shooters make the opposite adjustments.

*Legend
CR—Compound release-aid
CF—Compound fingers-release
RF—Recurve fingers-release

Use the information in this sidebar until you achieve a perfect arrow slit. If paper tuning remains unsatisfactory, despite the troubleshooting tips, then it's likely your arrow spine is off or the bow's cam rollover is faulty. If after trying several arrow spines and readjusting wheel rollover the poor arrow tears persist, then have your bow inspected by a professional archery shop.

Step No. 9
Verify Fletching Clearance

When using a drop-away rest, to verify proper arrow clearance, spray the rear-portion of the arrow with foot-powder spray. A smear indicates fletching contact, which will ruin arrow tune and accuracy.

This mainly applies to a release-aid set-up. Using a can of Desenex foot powder, spray the rear portion of the arrow (making sure the arrow's fletching is covered in the powdery film), and then shoot the arrow into a firm backstop (one that only allows the arrow to penetrate a few inches). Now look closely at the arrow to check for smear marks, mainly along the fletching. If you note contact, twist the arrow nock so the vanes are orientated in a different fashion. Continue to do this in 1/16-to-1/8-inch rotations, firing an arrow each time until the smear mark disappears.

Step No. 10
Paper Tuning With Fletched Arrow

Now is the time to check the real thing; how a fletched arrow comes out of the bow. Using taut paper, shoot a regular arrow from about 6 feet away. With a release-aid, you're looking for a clean three-slit tear and a small round circle, which makes up the arrow's footprint. This identifies perfect arrow flight. Very slight tears are acceptable, but you don't want anything more than that.

With a fingers release, a little bit of fletching tear from side to side is normal and acceptable.

BY JOE BELL

Fact: Exact cam rollover increases a bow's shooting forgiveness, accuracy and speed.

The next step is to reverify arrow flight by shooting into paper only, this time, further downrange. I do this by placing the paper at 15 feet, and then 10 yards. You should have a very clean arrow tear at all of these distances, even with a fingers release since arrow fletching and proper spine has now corrected any paradox/deviation in flight.

Once paper tuning is executed to perfection, your bow is ready to be sighted in and is also ready for broadhead shooting.

The final steps in paper tuning are shooting from 15 feet and then 10 yards. At these distances, you should achieve a clean arrow tear every time. Then it's time to sight-in your bow and begin shooting broadheads.

TECH TIPS

Troublesome Right Tear

With a release-aid, sometimes you'll have a slight tail-right tear regardless of what adjustments you make to the rest. This kind of tear can cause you to lose your hair. However, stay cool. When this happens, the cause can be narrowed to one of two things: Slight vane contact is occurring between the arrow rest's drop arm and fletching; or the bow has poor nock travel because of an excessive cam lean or faulty synchronization.

To fix the vane contact, speed up the drop time of the arrow rest arm and/or use shorter vanes, which will increase the time that the fletching has to pass. You can also mount the vanes slightly more rearward to accentuate this.

If clearance seems good but tail-right tear persists, then something is wrong with the bow's nock travel, particularly its horizontal travel. Double check wheel alignment and synchronization once again. If all else fails have the bow inspected by a certified pro shop mechanic or, better yet, the bow's manufacturer. A good bow will tune fairly easy when following this 10-step tune process.

Chapter 4
Arrow Performance

Choosing the Best Projectile for the Job

"Knowledge is more than equivalent to force."
—Samuel Johnson

Darin Cooper believes in heavier arrows for hunting. He typically shoots a 420-to-460-grain arrow. After crunching numbers and performing in-depth testing, he's come to the conclusion that momentum, not kinetic energy, is a better indicator of how well an arrow will penetrate. According to his tests and calculations, he's discovered that 50 grains of arrow weight is equivalent to shooting a 10-pound heavier bow when momentum is taken into account.

The arrow is a critical component of your bow set-up. Not only is it the "killing" part of the system, but it determines your shooting accuracy and flight trajectory. Top quality arrow shafts are uniform in spine, straightness and weight. This is vital for spot-on shooting, particularly with fixed-blade heads.

To ensure this kind of consistency, simply buy premium-labeled arrows or those with the tightest tolerances within their class, which correspond mainly to all-carbon shafts. Sure, they cost a little more, but these shafts are pre-sorted for consistency, so each shaft in a dozen bundle will be nearly exact to the next one, which translates into better shots. Whereas, if you buy lower-quality shafts, three or four in the dozen may never group, rendering them useless for anything other than flinging into a hillside.

Aluminum/carbon or all-aluminum shafts are a superb choice, considering these shafts are very precise right from the get-go because of their precise manufacturing process.

Beyond shaft consistency, however, you'll find an equally important issue, which isn't talked about as much. That is…the subject of shaft weight.

Fact: Heavier arrows always fly with more energy compared to lighter ones.

Speed will always be a big buzzword in the world of archery, just like it is in the gun industry. Some guys are convinced, the faster the arrow—or the bullet—the better you'll be at killing stuff. I disagree. The big compromise I see to ultra-fast arrow speed is the use of a super-light arrow. In my mind, light arrows hinder killing performance, big time. Here's why.

Need for Penetration

If you bowhunt less-than-hardy animals, such as pronghorn antelope, blacktail deer or smallish whitetails, then your 330-grain 3-D arrow remains a sensible choice. I say screw on some proven broadheads, sight-in, and go hunting.

However, mature whitetail bucks, along with mule deer and elk, are hardy 200-plus-pound critters. Sure, a clean, up-close broadside or slightly quartering-away shot offers an unencumbered path to the vitals. Nearly any arrow choice blows right on through.

But, when you start adding more animal angle and longer shots to the equation, the energy requirements change to achieve adequate penetration. In a nutshell, you need all the arrow wallop you can get to ensure a pass-through of the vitals. With big deer, mere inches of penetration could mean the difference between a quick kill and zero recovery.

Bell insists on shooting fairly heavy arrows for his big-game hunting, particularly for downrange energy. At long range, his 400-grain carbon arrow achieved full penetration on this trophy class elk.

In my experience, light arrows simply don't have the force to handle such situations each and every time, particularly when heavy bone is struck.

Just a few months ago I went elk hunting and shot a big New Mexico bull at approximately 10 yards. The animal came to a well-blown cow call and stopped sharply quartering-to from nearly 8 yards away and stared right at me. I had no shot. I decided since the shot was so close, I would shoot as soon as he turned to run. I did, and the arrow entered the chest perfectly, about four inches behind the shoulder crease.

Long story short, the arrow penetrated about 18 inches, using an ultra-sharp three-blade G5 Striker fixed-blade broadhead. As the animal walked off, I realized something went wrong. Because of the arrow probably hitting bone while at the same time the animal was twisting at high speed, penetration was greatly hindered. However, my 390-grain arrow went far enough to take one lung, the liver and split the diaphragm all the way to the off side. I recovered that bull; with a light arrow, I may have gotten only one lung, and likely no recovery of the animal.

That's just one instance where arrow weight can make the difference. Every inch of penetration can count in some situations, such as this one.

According to Randy Ulmer, "Light arrows are a mistake if you're not extremely selective in shot placement," he said. "Unless you are self-disciplined enough to take only broadside shots, then I would recommend against using them. Marginal shots are where they become a problem. I personally use a medium-weight arrow."

Fact: Maximum penetration, not speed, is the key to lethal hunting arrow performance.

It appears an arrow's Kinetic Energy output is the fundamental way to determine its penetrating ability, minus the factor of broadhead selection of course. To prove the heavier-arrow-is-better point, let's examine two arrows, a light vs. a medium-weight arrow, and see what the numbers conclude.

The Test: Light vs. Medium-Weight Shaft

Fact No. 1: Light arrows *always* deliver less energy compared to heavier ones. To prove this, let's take two arrows that fly great from the same bow but weigh differently (one is about 80 grains heavier). Both were spined correctly for the bow. Here are the arrow speeds and energy values.

The light arrow (340 grains) shot 279 fps, the heavier arrow (425 grains) 256 fps—a 23 fps difference. That's a substantial difference and the faster arrow will no doubt make you a better shooter on the 3-D course.

Slightly heavier arrows produce more momentum downrange, and they fly with greater stability in the wind. Bell shot this buck at long range, yet he knew his 400-grain arrow would penetrate deeply.

However, let's plug in these arrow weights and arrow speeds into the kinetic energy formula, which is: Velocity (squared) x Arrow Weight divided by 450,240 = Kinetic Energy in foot-pounds.

The light arrow: 77841 x 343 divided by 450,240 = 59.30 foot-pounds. The heavier arrow: 65536 x 426 divided by 450,240 = 62 foot-pounds. The difference: 2.7 foot-pounds. Obviously, this is not significant, but even then the energy difference is close to 5 percent, and that's measured right out of the bow!

Now let's look at what really matters in bowhunting—downrange power. At 40 yards, the light arrow travels at 265 fps, the heavier arrow 245 fps. Now, the light arrow has slowed down 15 fps, compared to 10 fps of the heavier arrow since the time of takeoff.

TECH TIPS

Formula for Kinetic Energy Velocity (squared) x Arrow Weight ÷ 450,240 = Kinetic Energy (in foot-pounds)

Formula for Momentum Momentum = (mass x velocity) ÷ 225,218 (in pounds-force x second)

At 40 yards, the light arrow offers 53.49 foot-pounds of energy, whereas the heavier arrow packs in 56.79 foot-pounds. The difference now is 3.3 foot-pounds, which equals to about 7 percent more energy. The significance is going up, and it intensifies more and more as the distance increases.

When bowhunting the West, 40-to-50-yard shots are common when pursuing mule deer, mountain goat or sheep, caribou and sometimes elk in open country. This kind of energy difference can save the day by punching clear through a deer, giving you two gaping broadhead holes, instead of just one, for an easy recovery.

Also, our test here involves only a "slightly" heavier arrow—a light vs. a medium-weight shaft. Take this test to an extreme level and the energy differences become more significant. For example, when comparing a 500-grain vs. a 300-grain arrow, the difference in energy output is about 8 or 9 percent at 40 yards. At 50 and 60 yards, the energy output opens up to 10 percent or more.

Momentum and Angled Hits

The author's good friend, Ron Way, arrowed this massive free-ranging California wild boar using a 410-grain arrow and a Snyper broadhead. Penetration was excellent.

Trying to shed some light on the factor of arrow weight and momentum, I performed a test several years ago in which I shot a few different arrows into a sheet of plywood. The plywood was positioned at a 60-degree angle and shot from 20 yards. Using various broadheads, it became obvious that a heavier arrow could make a difference on angled hits.

Each time, the heavier 450-grain arrow penetrated reliably whereas the lighter 340-grain arrow ricocheted off the board. Plywood is not an animal, but it's rather rigid like a shoulder bone on a deer or elk, so some reasonable conclusions can be drawn from this test. Although this examination was far from formal, it reinforced my decision to use heavier arrow set-ups in the woods.

"I believe super-light hunting arrows are a poor choice when hunting big animals," says my good friend Ron Way, who is an experienced bowhunter, broadhead designer, and aerospace engineer. "First off, medium-to-heavy-weight arrows will always stabilize (fly without wobbling) more rapidly when exiting a bow."

"Secondly is an important factor known as straight-line energy. Physics tell us that the more mass a body has, the harder it is for it to change directions, such as when an arrow strikes bone," notes Way. "Basically, lighter arrows have a greater ability to veer off target, whereas heavier arrows have less."

Darin Cooper shared his thoughts with me on this topic, too. "I definitely think archers shooting less than 400 grains on an elk or even mule deer and northern whitetails are asking for trouble regardless of arrow velocity," says Cooper. "I've done some engineering calculations that indicate how critical mass is to maximizing penetration. My calculations show that 50 grains of arrow weight is equivalent to shooting a 10-pound heavier bow… In other words, a 500-grain arrow shot from a 60-pound bow will achieve roughly the

same penetration as a 70-pound bow with a 450-grain arrow. The key is momentum and not kinetic energy."

"We got handed down kinetic energy as a measurement from the firearms industry—they're concerned about knock-down power, kinetic shockwaves, and bullet expansion for a projectile that's designed to stop in the animal," says Cooper. "Hydraulic shock and energy transfer is highly velocity dependent. Our killing efficiency is determined by how far the object will penetrate and cut tissue. The laws of physics dictate that when comparing two identically shaped objects in motion with equivalent momentum, one being heavier and the other faster, the heavier object will always travel farther (out-penetrate), because it has derived more of its momentum from mass."

TECH TIPS

A Better Team: Heavier Shafts and Fixed-Blade Broadheads

A large aircraft flies with greater stability compared to a small one, and so does a heavier arrow over a lighter one. If you like the reliability and performance of fixed-blade broadheads and get really tired of dealing with erratic broadhead flight, switch to a slightly heavier arrow and you'll most likely enjoy better flight and accuracy.

The arrow takeoff process with heavier arrows is simply slower and smoother, resulting in added shot forgiveness and easier tuning. Lighter arrows tend to fly out of the bow faster and more violently, and the slightest flaw in handle torque or tuning can cause the arrow to whip off course, steering fixed-blade heads right out of the sweet spot.

With lighter arrows, the usual solution is to switch to an ultra-small fixed head or a mechanical broadhead. This is a compromise you may not want.

Bruce Barrie, of Rocky Mountain Broadheads, has hunted a lot with a variety of arrow weights. With light arrows, although he likes their speed, he's had a few penetration problems occur over the years. For example, Barrie made a perfect shot on this Montana whitetail with a 330-grain arrow and fixed-blade broadhead, only the broadhead and arrow ricocheted off bone and penetrated toward the paunch, even though the animal was facing slightly quartering away at the hit.

Cooper adds, "I typically shoot a 420-to-460-grain arrow. When I finally figure out how to get a 500-grain arrow to shoot 280 fps at my draw length and draw weight, I'll do it. If I ever do a moose, or grizzly hunt, I'll be packing arrows that weigh 550-to-650 grains."

Combining Speed with Punch!

For maximum energy and shot forgiveness you should choose the heaviest arrow possible. However, a very heavy arrow hinders arrow speed and your chances of hitting animals at unknown distances. The solution is simple: choose a shaft that's not too heavy and not too light—a medium-weight contender. These shafts, in my mind, make the optimal choice, since they give you the best of both worlds—speed, along with downrange energy.

The easiest way to figure out what a "medium weight" shaft is for your set-up is to look at Easton's Arrow Sizing Chart. Easton offers a wide selection of shafts, from very heavy

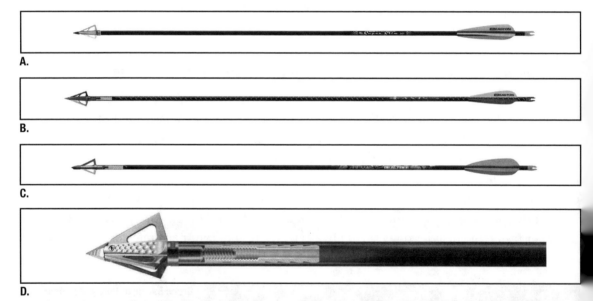

Three great medium-weight arrow choices are: a. the Easton A/C Super Slim (9.7 grains per inch – 400 size), b. Easton Axis Full Metal Jacket (9.9 grains per inch) and c. Beman Team Realtree MFX (9.6 grains per inch). All these shafts utilize Hidden Insert Technology, which creates better broadhead alignment (d).

to very light, all within just one arrow spine size. Look at the choices in the middle of this spectrum—these are mid-weight shafts.

Generally speaking, shafts that weigh about 6 grains for every pound of bow-pull weight offer a nice blend of arrow speed, downrange kinetic energy, and fixed-blade flying stability.

An easier calculation is to look at the arrow's grains-per-inch weight, which most

The Carbon Express Terminator Hunter is another excellent midweight arrow shaft.

manufacturer's label clearly on the shaft. Personally, I prefer bare arrow shafts that weigh 9 grains per inch or more. My set-up specs are 27- to 28-inch draw (depending on whether I'm shooting release or fingers), 70-pound pull, and a 26-to-27-inch arrow. Usually my shafts weigh from 380-to-440 grains. My favorite set-up at this time is the Easton Super Slim 400 (9.7 grains per inch) or Easton Full Metal Jacket 400 (9.9 grains per inch) and a 100-grain broadhead. Total arrow weight is 390 grains and 430 grains, respectively.

Fact: Mid-weight arrows offer the perfect blend of speed, accuracy, quiet bow performance, and penetrating power.

Other Pros

Beyond its capability to penetrate better, a medium-weight arrow yields other favorable qualities. One important factor is "forgiveness," and this holds true whether you use fixed or mechanical broadheads. There's a good reason why indoor target shooters use the heaviest arrows and point-combinations spined correctly for their bows. The goal: To create shafts that are as stable and forgiving as possible. The objective in this game is to hit the X-ring each and every time at 18 meters and these oversize, super-heavy 500-to-600-grain "logs" maximize this effort.

Heavier arrows produce a quieter shot, and they shoot more accurately, particularly when you shoot from awkward positions in the field.

TECH TIPS

Insist on Arrow Precision

Carbon arrows dominate the market yet these same shafts are more prone to irregular spine, which is essentially the measured "flex rate" of a shaft. Of course, top-end carbon arrows are usually sorted for consistent spine, which eliminates the fear of poorly spined arrows. But with low to mid-grade shafts, this isn't always the case and it's wise to check each arrow's spine value. For good accuracy, arrows shouldn't vary more than .010-inch in spine, and for shooting fixed-blade broadheads at high speeds it should vary even less than that.

A new product called the Carbon QC Spine Tester makes this otherwise-tedious procedure a breeze. Simply adjust the jig to match your arrow size, attach the included weight, and look at the micro-dial to see the spine value. This tool works equally well with any other shaft material. This device allows you to do other things as well, such as check the concentricity of your broadheads (to an amazing .0005-inch, plus or minus) and to precisely index arrow nocks to the stiffest portion of the shaft for the tightest possible groups.

Contact Ram Products, 1220 S. Mountain View Rd., Moscow, ID 83843; (208) 882-1396 or www.ram-products.com.

The author finds slightly heavier arrows to group better, day in and day out, particularly at 60 yards and further.

A heavier hunting arrow will shoot more forgiving and accurately for the same reason. Because of sheer weight and slower launch speeds, it is more stable and less likely to be "thrown" off target thanks to a minor release or follow-through flaw. I urge you to switch to a heavier arrow and do your own testing. Despite less-than-perfect archery form, heavier arrows seem to stay on target. This characteristic is especially useful when you're faced with high-adrenaline, high-pressure shots in the field. A fast arrow may be a blessing on the 3-D range, but a slower, heavier arrow counts for more in a tree stand when you've got the jitters and crunch time has arrived.

I was reminded of this forgiveness factor when doing these velocity tests. My chronograph has a rather

---

TECH TIPS

Did You Know...? Small-Diameter Arrows Offer More Advantages

Arrow shafts that have smaller diameters require less fletching to rotate in flight. This makes shorter, lighter fletching like New Archery's QuikSpin Hunter a more sensible choice.

Arrow-makers preach about two primary advantages in shooting a smaller-diameter carbon-arrow shaft—penetration (because of friction) and less wind drift. Certainly, these are great factors to have working in your favor. However, there's a hidden advantage few think of when shooting a "skinnier" arrow shaft. The most important is the control factor inherent in these shafts.

By talking to engineers on the subject, I've come to realize that for every decrease in shaft diameter, the faster that shaft will spin using the same fletch and helical.

For example, let's take three different shaft-diameter sizes. A large 2315 aluminum (measures about 11/32-inch wide), a typical internal-component carbon

arrow shaft (about 5/16-inch wide), and one of the new Easton AXIS or Beman MFX Team Realtree HIT shafts (about 17/64-inch wide).

Now, if we were to outfit each of these arrows with vanes mounted at a 5-degree helical, the spin rates would vary for each shaft. For every one full rotation, the 2315 would have to travel forward 8.8 inches, the 5/16-inch carbon 7.99 inches and the skinny 17/64-inch carbon 6.8 inches! (Because of variables such as wind and drag, these numbers are relative not actual.)

The premise, according to aerospace engineers, is that ultra small-diameter shafts have a smaller axis of rotation. This means smaller fletching or less vane helical (angle) is needed to get the arrow spinning so that air drag is produced for flying stability.

This spinning and air drag is known as centrifugal force. Basically, think of a simple tabletop. When you spin it slow, it tends to wobble. But if you spin it faster, it builds up air resistance or drag and becomes stable; the wobbling stops. The arrow requires the same—it must spin fast enough so that fletching creates the right amount of air drag to make it stable in flight.

In the end, this means smaller-diameter arrows not only give us improved flight trajectory downrange (because of less surface area and drag), but they give us the ability to use smaller vanes or less vane helical without theoretically sacrificing loss of arrow stability or control.

Darin Cooper's Momentum Chart: Heavy vs. Medium-Weight Arrow

Heavy-weight arrow, 70-pound bow, 29-inch draw

	70# 29" 500gr				60# 29" 500gr		
	Velocity fps	KE ft-lb$_f$	Momentum lb$_f$-s		Velocity fps	KE ft-lb$_f$	Momentum lb$_f$-s
Initial	265.0	78.0	0.588		248.0	68.3	0.551
20 yards	257.9	73.8	0.573		241.3	64.6	0.536
30 yards	254.5	71.9	0.565		238.0	62.9	0.528
40 yards	251.0	69.9	0.557		234.7	61.2	0.521
50 yards	247.7	68.1	0.550		231.5	59.5	0.514
60 yards	244.3	66.3	0.542		228.3	57.9	0.507
70 yards	241.0	64.5	0.535		225.2	56.3	0.500
80 yards	237.7	62.7	0.528		222.1	54.8	0.493

Medium-weight arrow, 70-pound bow, 29-inch draw

	70# 29" 450gr				60# 29" 450gr		
	Velocity fps	KE ft-lb$_f$	Momentum lb$_f$-s		Velocity fps	KE ft-lb$_f$	Momentum lb$_f$-s
Initial	276.0	76.1	0.551		258.0	66.5	0.516
20 yards	267.9	71.7	0.535		250.3	62.6	0.500
30 yards	264.0	69.6	0.527		246.6	60.8	0.493
40 yards	260.0	67.5	0.519		242.8	58.9	0.485
50 yards	256.2	65.6	0.512		239.2	57.2	0.478
60 yards	252.4	63.7	0.504		235.6	55.5	0.471
70 yards	248.6	61.7	0.497		232.0	53.8	0.464
80 yards	244.9	59.9	0.489		228.5	52.2	0.457

small 10-inch square-triangle-like shooting tunnel. At 40 yards, it looks about 5 inches wide. With the heavier arrows, I knew I'd thread the eye of the needle. With the lighter arrows, I had some twitchy doubts, though I got them all through. Still, mentally, it was different, and bowhunting is a very mental pursuit.

Heavier arrows are quieter, too. Go ahead and deck out your bow with all the latest sound-dampening accessories hoping for the quietest shot possible. But realize that a heavier arrow will always emit a duller thud at the shot. This ultra-quiet thud could get you a second shot, just in case you need it. That's a big deal.

Finally, heavier arrows—whether all carbon, carbon/aluminum or all-aluminum—are usually more durable and simply last longer. When you "slap" arrows together, ultra-light arrows tend to fracture more easily and become a constant nuisance. Heavier arrows keep you less worried and shooting more, whether it is at targets or dirt clumps and stumps as you "plink" your way back into elk camp.

Bottom Line

Light arrows may rule for 3-D shooting, but don't make them your first choice for bowhunting big deer or larger big game that simply require more downrange punch. By all means use light, accurate arrows during the spring and summer when 3-D tournaments are a great way to sharpen your archery skills. But be wise and make the switch back to a more reliable heavier arrow set-up. As long as you give yourself a month or two of time to familiarize yourself with this slower set-up's trajectory, you'll find yourself no less confident come hunting time.

Besides, your laser rangefinder will tell you the exact distance to your buck or bull on 90 percent of your shots. From here the job is simple: execute a good shot. Your "beefy" arrow choice will take care of the rest. The numbers tell us so.

Fact: Effective mid-weight arrows weigh around 9 grains or more per inch of shaft weight.

TECH TIPS

Obtaining Arrow Stability: FOC Specs

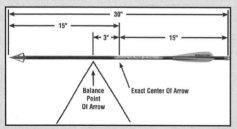

Proper arrow front of center (FOC) weight is necessary for downrange accuracy, particularly when it's windy out. The author recommends shooting 10 percent or more weight.

An arrow's front of center (FOC) weight is critical for optimum flight stability downrange, especially when the wind bucks. Easton recommends 10 percent or more weight forward for optimum control. With smaller, lighter vanes or feathers, it's now easier than ever to achieve a higher FOC.

If you've ever flown in a small aircraft or a commercial airliner, you know from experience that the larger plane flies so much more smoothly and, thus, with more stability. Consider arrows in the same light. Structurally speaking, ultra-light arrows are naturally less stable in flight. This is why you shouldn't drop arrow weight too much to gain arrow speed.

Now is also a good time to address the issue of sufficient arrow length. In the past, arrows shorter than 26 inches were said to be less stable in flight versus longer arrows. This is another reason why bowhunters using extra-long overdraws achieved poor arrow flight with broadheads.

What affects stability in this case, some engineers suggest, is the distance between the center-weight of the arrow and the fletching. The shorter the distance between this central balancing point and the weight of the fletching, the less stable the arrow tends to be.

I'm not convinced this is entirely true, since shaft weight is another critical component that determines flight stability. However, assuming this center-weight factor is true, with the use of today's well-designed short fletching, one could say that arrow lengths can be a bit shorter without sacrificing stability. You can cut down arrows to about 24 or 25 inches without losing much arrow control.

BY JOE BELL

Chapter 5
The Best Broadhead

The Tip Does All the Work – Get it Right

"The most successful people in life are generally those who have the best information."
—Benjamin Disraeli

Randy Ulmer was never overly impressed with the performance of expanding-blade broadheads until the Rocky Mountain Snyper came along. He quickly was won over by its fail-proof, deep-penetrating design. Today he uses the Rage, which is based on the same cam-opening blade concept.

One of my most memorable shots to date happened in the mountains of Northwest Territories, Canada. A lot of preparation, time, money and hard walking went into this hunt, and finally a shooting opportunity was before me. As I sneaked in from above, with a cliff separating the standing mountain caribou and me, I knew I'd be faced with a tricky shot angle.

I stared nearly straight down at the giant bull. As I looked over the angle intently, I thought about how I had honed my equipment all year long to handle the toughest shots. I was using a fairly heavy small-diameter Easton A/C Super Slim arrow and an ultra-tough, ultra-accurate fixed three-blade broadhead. My bow was shooting incredibly well.

With confidence strong, I decided I could pinpoint my arrow right down through the bull's vitals from about 25 yards.

Soon, my arrow was on its way, speeding along its course. I watched in surprise as the arrow penetrated nearly to the fletching. After trotting 100 yards or so, the bull staggered to the ground and expired.

Every bowhunter should have 100-percent confidence in the broadhead he is using. The reality in bowhunting is that shot angles don't always end up being perfect, even when you do your very best to set up good shots. In many ways, your success afield comes down to that little sharp thing on the front of the arrow. Choose the right one and you could be a hero. Choose the wrong one, and serious gloom can consume you once that trophy buck or bull bolts away after the hit, never to be found again.

In my mind, to make lethal, successful kills under tough field conditions, a broadhead must perform four important functions. It must: 1. Fly with great accuracy 2. Cut a lethal hole using ultra-sharp blades 3. Stay intact when encountering bone and continue to cut if the arrow stays in the animal 4. Penetrate deeply in a straight line from its course of entry, regardless of somewhat sharp-angled impacts.

Accuracy

Even the smallest broadhead kills fast when bisecting the animal's lungs, whereas the largest broadhead shot into the paunch kills by slow, agonizing death from infection. The point is obvious—a good hunting broadhead is an extremely accurate broadhead that can get the job done.

Unfortunately, our shots don't always go where we want them to, so a large-cutting head, which creates a larger wound channel and more tissue devastation, and one that flies straight to the target, is the optimum choice.

BY JOE BELL

Mike Slinkard prefers the reliability of compact fixed-blade heads. Besides, from an accuracy standpoint, he doesn't see the advantage of a mechanical head. He regularly shoots field-point size groups with his fixed heads, even out to 80 yards or so. The key, he says, is proper head-to-shaft alignment.

The big hindrance to broadhead accuracy is arrow speed—too much of it causes steering problems. Fast arrows simply go better with smaller broadheads. Here are my recommendations on maximum broadhead size based on arrow speed and ensuring your heads are ready for the field.

Head/Speed Recommendations: Generally speaking, if you shoot beyond 270 fps, don't waste your time with heads with cutting diameters larger than 1 3/16-inch and that have blades longer than about ¾-inch. Choose today's more compact fixed-style heads much like the Rocky Mountain Ti-100 or Innerloc 100.

Accuracy Test: When testing a broadhead for accuracy, I screw on three heads (precisely seated/aligned to the shafts) and begin group shooting from 40 or 50 yards. If the heads veer more than a few inches from my field points, I try a different brand. I paper tune my bows precisely and want my well-matched broadheads to easily group inside five or six inches at 40 yards and close to the impact of my field points.

Fact: Small broadheads are effective at killing game, but with marginal hits, their deadliness becomes questionable.

When shooting beyond 270 fps, I seem to achieve great consistency with compact fixed-style heads, such as the Muzzy 4-blade 90 or 100-grain, G5 Striker, Rocky Mountain Blitz, Slick Trick 1-inch, or Innerloc Stainless Extreme 100, to name a few.

Rocky Mountain's Blitz (left) and G5's Striker are two excellent high-speed fixed-blade heads to choose from.

Acceptable Accuracy: Accurate fixed-blade broadheads will group in nearly the same fashion as field points. When I'm feeling good, I expect to shoot 4-to-5-inch three-arrow groups at 50 yards using my broadheads. Don't accept anything less than top-notch accuracy from your hunting heads.

"In calm conditions I think a well-tuned, high-quality fixed-blade head can group almost as good as a mechanical," says pro archer Darin Cooper. "The biggest issue is that a lot of bowhunters (and even pro shops) don't know how to perfectly match the arrow spine to their bow, or they don't spend the money on high-quality arrow shafts, or they can't tune a bow perfectly or execute the shot consistently. Mechanical broadheads are more forgiving of all of these sins."

TECH TIPS

Flight Hiss

Broadhead hiss can lead to animals "jumping the string," where the animal darts, ducks, or springs out of the way at the moment of release, which can cause poor hits or misses. The best way to detect broadhead hiss is to place a friend about 30 yards downrange from a 40-yard target. Make sure he's safely off to the side and perhaps protected by a barrier of some sort. Have him listen for any audible hum as you fire a few arrows into the target. Insist on quiet broadhead flight, no exceptions.

Cutting Surface

The author used a G5 Striker broadhead to bring down this New Mexico bull.

For devastating wound channels, I prefer broadheads that offer about 2 ½-to-close to 3 inches of well-honed cutting surface. These same heads also come with fairly wide cutting widths. Broadheads vary too much in design to label what's a legitimate cutting width in one category or another. I will say this, though: Heads with one-inch cuts are a marginal choice, unless they sport 4 blades. A smallish, 1-inch wide (or less) three-blade broadhead tends to cut a slit-like hole, whereas, in my opinion, a top quality 1-inch wide four-blade head (such as the Muzzy 100 or Slick Trick) cuts a small hole, but one that gapes open, so blood can flow out. There's a considerable difference in performance with the addition of another sharp-cutting blade.

Cutting surface, and not just the hole a broadhead cuts, is important for this reason: When shot into an animal, a broadhead must pass through several blade-dulling layers. First, it passes through hair, hide, exterior meat and likely rib bone. Then it makes its way through vital tissue, which is slick and somewhat rubbery in nature but contains various blood vessels.

Only a really sharp edge will cleanly snip these tiny cylinders of blood. Also, if something less than a razor-sharp instrument bisects lung tissue, then the chance increases for what's known as localized blunt trauma. In this case, dull blades cut tissue, but swelling occurs, blood flow is scanty or non-existent, and the injury seals up.

"The more blade area you have the harder it is to get the broadhead through an animal," says Bob Mizek, director of engineering for New Archery Products. "Blade area involves all blade surface areas, including the sides of the blades as well. This allows compact broadheads to penetrate exceedingly well, perhaps better than mid-size offerings.

"But if you're going to use a short head, it had better be sharp—and I mean sharp from start to finish—otherwise killing effectiveness can suffer," says Mizek. "Broadheads with longer cutting edges, even when slightly dulled, will cause more damage. Considering all of his, a midsize broadhead like the

TECH TIPS

Broadhead Alignment

This is the critical part. The broadhead must spin absolutely true when attached to the arrow—there can't be any wobble along the ferrule, or at the front of the arrow or the insert base. A slight deviation in the broadhead's tip area is probably okay, but I still like to choose heads with ultra-straight bodies—from the very base to the top of the tip—for the best possible aerodynamics.

To check alignment, buy a Pine Ridge arrow spinner and look for any wobble as the arrow and broadhead rotate in fast revolutions. Few broadheads spin perfectly with just any shaft. This occurs because of imprecise inserts or insert installation. You might have to try mounting several different broadheads onto different shafts until you get it right. With aluminum or ACC type arrows, heating and twisting inserts (when hot-melt glue is used) or switching out inserts can solve this problem as well.

With carbon arrows, the only real alternative is to use G5's ASD tool to create a perfectly flush face on the arrow's insert or the arrow's tip (in the case of Easton's or Beman's HIT style arrows). This tool is a big time saver and maximizes the performance of every carbon arrow on hand.

If arrow wobble continues, then save that shaft and possibly the broadhead for occasional plinking, nothing else.

Mike Slinkard, a pro-level archer, bowhunter, and owner of Winner's Choice Custom Bowstrings, takes broadhead alignment seriously. He says without it he can't achieve the kind of field-point-like accuracy he requires.

"I have an old aluminum arrow straightener with a meter gauge that I can place directly on the arrow's insert," said Slinkard. "With this tool, I can detect the slightest bit of off alignment. Basically, I switch out inserts and try new broadheads until all my broadheads are perfectly aligned to the insert—with a degree of accuracy of 1/1000th of an inch. This step really helps to tighten my arrow groups, and my hunting heads hit right along with my field points.

"Most of my hunting bows shoot arrows around 280 fps," adds Slinkard. "I have had a few that shot over 300 fps as well. Again, perfect head alignment is what will make or break accuracy especially at heightened arrow speed. One of the most accurate hunting bows I have ever owned shot my hunting arrows at 304 fps. My only problem with that bow was a short brace height that gave me arm clearance problems when wearing heavy clothing.

"I want my broadheads to group nearly as well as my field points," he noted. "This type of accuracy sometimes takes many hours of tuning the arrow rest, but the end result is absolute optimum accuracy and confidence when faced with a difficult shot. Also, this ensures that the arrow is impacting the animal with its maximum amount of power that only comes from perfect arrow flight."

Thunderhead 100 or slightly smaller Thunderhead XP is perhaps a safer all-around bet. Generally speaking, manufacturers are better able to design mid-size heads and build them using high-quality materials. Also, most importantly, with these heads there's enough length to the blades to divide up the work so the job is done more effectively."

A broadhead can only kill quickly in two ways—through massive hemorrhaging (vast amounts of bleeding), or what is known as asphyxiation, where the animal quickly suffocates because of the deflating of the lungs. A dull broadhead won't cause massive amounts of bleeding, and it won't create a gaping, non-sealing hole in a deer's lungs. If either of these critical outcomes does not occur, there's a great chance the deer will live long enough to escape your follow-up or recovery.

Heads with little actual cutting surface dull more easily compared to those with more cutting volume. This makes them less effective at putting down game.

Durability/Strength

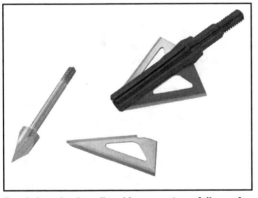

Fuse's Innerloc broadhead incorporates a fail-proof blade-locking system.

Broadhead durability is of great importance because the moment a broadhead falls apart, it stops cutting. Big deer and elk-size game are tough customers, and solid hits in bone can force some broadheads to roll back like a banana peel, causing nothing more than a superficial wound.

I once shot a bull moose with a prototype fixed-blade three-blade head touted as a deep-penetrating design. I pulled it from the side of the moose because it never exited the other side, and I noticed all three blades and the tip were missing. Fortunately, the arrow did enough damage before it failed.

Durability is also important to consider for another reason: religious practice. I shoot broadheads throughout the winter, spring and summer. I also shoot every head I hunt with a few times in a foam target to ensure point-on accuracy, then I change out the blades. Heads that are made from flimsy, low-quality aluminum are one-shot wonders that won't hold up to rigorous pre-hunt practice. In most cases, the ferrules will bend after one or two shots, and once that happens, shooting consistency takes a serious dive.

Fact: Good blood trails rarely exist without adequate broadhead penetration.

This is why I favor all-steel or titanium ferrules, or proven aluminum ferrules from companies such as New Archery, Innerloc, Magnus, Muzzy or Rocky Mountain.

Also, I prefer heads that I can actually stump-shoot with during the course of the season. The heads that hold up well to this abuse only help to increase my peace of mind on big game.

As a final analysis, I shoot a few of the broadheads I like through sheet metal, about 1/8-inch thick. This test sheds light on how well a broadhead will stay intact, particularly its blades, during the course of a hard hit. Any indication of blades dislodging or snapping off makes me doubt the head's effectiveness if heavy bone was struck.

Penetration

Bell made a precise hit on this big mountain caribou. He had great confidence in taking the shot, since he was using an accurate and ultra-sturdy fixed-blade broadhead.

Aside from arrow energy, two things determine how well a broadhead penetrates:

1. Overall design of the broadhead's ferrule and tip; and

2. Length and number of cutting blades and the degree of the blade slope. In simple terms, the less surface area and blades a broadhead has, the better it penetrates.

Most of today's broadheads penetrate well, but many fail miserably when angled shots are in the equation. An effective broadhead drives deep, regardless of a slight angle, inline from its point of entry. If not, serious deflection can occur, causing poor hits and possible non-recovery of the animal, despite good placement of the arrow.

Blade angle is a bigger issue than most think. Simply put, the stronger the angle, the greater the chance for arrow/broadhead deflection.

As previously mentioned, years ago I did some informal testing using plywood positioned at a 60-degree angle (which is steep, but isn't excessive). I covered the board with a thin blanket to replicate animal hide and hair. Of course, plywood is far from the structure of an animal's chest, but in my mind this medium does offer some validity as to how broadheads would behave if they were to collide with heavy bone.

I shot my test arrows and broadheads from 20 yards, and the results were very noteworthy. Some broadheads hit the board and propelled off, while others skidded a bit before penetrating. And a few penetrated the moment they struck! All in all it was quite obvious to me that broadhead design can make a definite difference.

Although my test was far from a formal examination, I noticed some valuable tendencies among the heads tested. Usually, slender, ultra-sharp cutting-nose tipped broadheads resisted skidding along the blanket and plywood, digging in almost immediately upon hitting. Whereas, steep-bladed 3-blade style chisel-tip broadheads had the tendency to skid off the target material, skidding and cutting sideways. I will note that the G5 Montec was an exception. It penetrated successfully, which makes sense considering its knife-like tip.

Muzzy's 100-grain 4-Blade head is an excellent do-all design, according to the author.

I also came to the general conclusion that broadheads with abrupt blade angles penetrated poorly but models with identical tips and more-sloping blades penetrated successfully.

"When shot angles are very sharp, the blade on the broadhead can actually strike first or at the same time as the tip," says Bruce Barrie, past president and owner of Rocky Mountain Broadheads. "This is where blades that are attached at low angles have a benefit."

"However, in a real-world situation shooting at an animal, severe blade angles don't hinder penetration on sharply angled shots as much," Barrie adds. "Test board is solid and unforgiving. Animal tissue and rib cages, on the other hand, do give somewhat and the broadhead is likely to penetrate regardless. But even so, this test does shed some validity on ideal broadhead design."

Another point to mention is that most two-blade type broadheads do well under this kind of shooting circumstance, but their penetrating ability depends on the tip shape and how the blades are oriented upon hitting. In my tests, a vertical blade pattern seemed to dig in and penetrate, whereas a horizontal-blade orientation tended to skid.

Remember, this test is far from perfect. Two-blade broadheads are among the best-proven penetrators on game, likely the best, but on sharply angled shots they could have a small downside. However, I should note that two-blade heads with slender, ultra-sharp cutting noses didn't have a problem with penetrating the blanket and wood.

Heads with slimmer noses and less blade angle seem to excel in these tests. For this reason, I strive to go with a broadhead that offers the least amount of blade angle as possible, given it flies true. If not, sometimes I have to compromise based on my arrow speed.

Fixed Blade vs. Mechanical

TECH TIPS

Fletching: Use Just Enough

An effective arrow flies as fast as possible without losing flight or broadhead stability, which will affect point-on accuracy. This is where arrow fletching comes into play.

The fletching's job is to produce air drag and arrow spin, both of which produce flight stability. Too much drag slows the arrow down, affecting trajectory. Trajectory is important when you don't know the exact distance to the target, which is key when hunting rutting bucks or bulls, which don't seem to stand still.

So the trick here is to outfit your arrow with just enough fletching and helical (offset of fletching). Generally speaking, the greater the fletching's surface area, the greater the drag or control. The same goes for more rotational spin, or helical. However, too much of either slows down arrow speed and reduces trajectory—something you don't want. The key is to find the perfect blend for your particular arrow set-up.

The only way to do this is to experiment with different style fletching combinations. Start with standard 4-inch vanes and work your way down. I suggest at least a moderate helical, no matter what kind of broadhead or vanes you're using.

In my experience, however, today's short, tall, rigid vanes (my choice is the AAE Max Hunter) offer excellent arrow stability using everything but the largest broadheads. They work great with all arrow rests as well, since they optimize rest clearance, particularly with drop-away arrow rests.

The Slick Trick is a super-tough, super-accurate fixed head. The author has shot this head at high speed without accuracy issues. Its Alcatraz blade-locking system is uniquely designed and ensures no loss of blades.

I have nothing against mechanical broadheads; I use them from time to time, especially in windy, long-range conditions where they excel. However, I do believe they have problems.

The Rocky Mountain Snyper and Rage use a cam-opening blade concept rather than blades that swing outward to open. This concept eliminates the chance of deflection and practically eliminates all penetration loss when blades deploy open.

For starters, unlike a fixed-blade head, they are not built with strength first and foremost in mind. The blades on a mechanical head are only supported at one end, not along its entire length like a fixed-style head. This makes it a liability in the field in my mind, especially when tackling larger big game.

Many broadhead engineers tell me how their blades are heat-treated for strength and pliability, which makes them impossible to break and only bend during blows with bone. I have a hard time believing this; each year I see mechanical heads with snapped-off blades. Also, special heat treats require additional manufacturing costs and most companies aren't willing to spend the money.

Additionally, most mechanicals don't have reliable blade-deployment systems. This concern largely revolves around the amount of friction caused by the blades as they open on impact. Some retard penetration badly, others not much at all.

The author's good friend, CJ Davis, shot this bruiser Wisconsin buck using the Rage mechanical head. After harvesting six animals with this head—all clean, one-shot kills—he's thoroughly impressed with its performance.

My favorite mechanical heads are ones with cam-opening blades and ones with less abrupt blade angles, such as the Rocky Mountain Snyper. This head penetrates with little to no friction, penetrating like a fixed head. It's an awesome head and stands as my go-to mechanical head. It also produces great in-line, entry-hole penetration since most of the ferrule delves into flesh first before blades deploy.

I'm also fond of Rocket's Sidewinder broadhead though it's a "jack knife" style design. This head uses an elongated tip, which helps with in-line penetration and prevents cartwheeling.

BY JOE BELL

Bruce Barrie often hunts using the Rage two-blade head.

According to Randy Ulmer, "Basically, I hated mechanicals early on because they didn't work well. However, once I started shooting the Snyper, I was converted. You simply cannot shoot a fixed-blade broadhead as well as a mechanical. You cannot be as accurate; period."

Recently, Chuck Adams, who has criticized mechanical broadheads for years, is now using a mechanical head for all of his hunting. "Traditionally I've been skeptical of mechanicals," said Adams. "Even today, most mechanical heads waste too much energy upon impact and are too fragile. However, the Rage and Snyper pretty much cancel out those disadvantages.

"I believe mechanicals are advantageous in a good crosswind. The Rage and Snyper offer a slight advantage when you're cold or tired or the wind is blowing and the shot might not be a perfect shot. And for the average guy who's shooting a fast carbon arrow, mechanical heads are the only way to go, if, again you're using a good one. I would tackle any North American big-game animal with one of these heads."

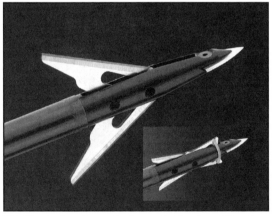

This illustration shows the Snyper in the closed (inset) and open position.

Personally, my main beef with mechanicals is this: I have seen occasional failure in blade capture during high-speed flight. Arrow speed alone won't cause blades to partially deploy. What causes it more than anything is rotational speed, or what engineers call centrifugal force. Some mechanical heads with weak rubber bands seem to accentuate partial deployment during flight, causing accuracy problems.

Fact: Not every mechanical broadhead works; some open in flight.

While conducting accuracy tests for this book, I noticed a severe hissing occurring with several different styles of mechanical heads. This made me further examine the cause. With a sheet of thin paper placed 40 yards down range and a firm backstop to stop the arrow before fletching passes through paper, I noticed the blades of these mechanical heads were indeed opening during flight. Once I placed two sets of rubber bands on the blades, the hissing went away, blades stayed closed, and group sizes shrunk.

My advice is to use extra-firm rubber bands or put two of them on to ensure blade placement. You must test all heads over and over for flight integrity. Remember, don't just check one head; check at least six.

Not all mechanical broadheads are accurate. These two groups were shot at 40 yards using a shooting machine. One three-arrow group is with field points, the other with mechanical heads. Afterward, the author discovered the heads were opening slightly in flight, causing the accuracy issue.

For archers who don't know how to tune a bow well, or simply shoot too much speed for long-range accuracy, consider choosing a quality mechanical head. Test these heads religiously before simply screwing them in and going hunting, though. To not test your equipment is irresponsible. Do some durability testing of your own and be sure to shoot the heads downrange through tissue paper and make sure they aren't prematurely opening. Mechanical heads that open in flight will produce horrible accuracy, much worse than most fixed-style heads from a non-tuned arrow.

"There's no question that mechanical broadheads simplify the set-up and tuning process for hunting shafts," explains Darin Cooper. "They also have an indisputable advantage when you consider wind drift. However, every mechanical broadhead robs some portion of the arrow's penetration to open the blades. They also have a tendency to kick the arrow on angled shots. That kick can substantially reduce penetration. I know of a lot of mechanical-head users who have passed on quartering shots that were well within their effective range due to the shot angle. I don't want to have to pass a shot to make an ethical and humane kill—I simply don't have time."

I can recall many moments where I worried excessively about broadhead performance, particularly as I followed up along a spotty blood trail. Nowadays, I rarely do that. I know my broadhead choice was the absolute best for my set-up, and if the blood trail just happens to be sparse, I know deep down inside the lack of blood isn't the broadhead's fault. Rather, the blame is likely on the archer and the placement of the arrow.

TECH TIPS

Blade Sharpness

Using a chunk of cowhide, I rub a broadhead blade with a light touch. If it doesn't cut immediately, it's not sharp enough. A super-sharp broadhead does more than you could ever know to cause excessive blood loss and quick kills.

I typically prefer replaceable broadhead blades. In side-by-side tests, these seem sharper. However, some heads with non-replaceable main blades, such as the Magnus Snuffer SS, are pretty darn sharp and resharpen very well.

BY JOE BELL

Chapter 6
Optimizing Accuracy

Facts and Myths Behind Shot-to-Shot Consistency

"The only way to find the limits of the possible is by going beyond them to the impossible."
—Arthur C. Clarke

Super-accurate arrow accuracy and bowhunting turkeys go hand in hand. The author had his Hoyt bow super-tuned for the task at hand.

When I began reloading rifle cartridges in my mid-teens, I realized true accuracy comes from trial and error, or intense experimentation. Every rifle has a "sweet spot" where it performs best using a specific type and amount of gunpowder, primer, bullet selection and seated height. Also, "free floating" a barrel and the receiver will typically accentuate this accuracy.

Your bow set-up is no different. By experimenting with different arrows, spine sizes, fletching, front of center specs, and broadheads, you'll eventually find the ultimate choice. However, the accuracy choice of a bow goes beyond its "ammo" or arrow choice. Since a lot of your body interacts with the bow when shooting, many variables affect accuracy, such as bow balance, add-on accessories and bowstring set-up. Here are some helpful tips on dialing in your bow for maximum accuracy.

No. 1:
Super Tune Your Bow

Long-range accuracy with fixed-blade broadheads comes by paying attention to the details. This three-arrow group was shot at 90 yards.

Creep Tuning: Creep tuning is a concept performed best with a two-cam bow, since it revolves around the synchronization of the cams. To do it, you simply shoot your bow at 20 yards, while aiming at a straight horizontal line (a piece of tape or edge of a target face). With your first arrow, you are to pull hard into the cam's wall and shoot. On the next shot, you are to creep so you shoot from the front-most portion of the bow's valley (opposite direction of the wall) and shoot arrow number 2. Of course, you rule out bad shots when doing this. The premise being, if your bow's eccentrics are properly timed then your arrows should both end up somewhere along the tape (side to side). Now, if the "creep" shot hits high, you are to shorten the cable that connects to the bottom cam. If it hits low, then you are to shorten the cable that connects to the top cam. You make minute adjustments until arrows hit on the same horizontal plane.

Tiller Tuning: This works on all styles of bows, including those with hybrid cams or single-cam designs. To perform it, simply shoot at various targets at a distance at which you're comfortable shooting tight groups. From here, you shoot a group of 3 or 4 arrows, then simply turn the top limb ¼-turn at a time, shooting a group of arrows at each juncture, until you've turned the limb bolt one full turn. It's a good

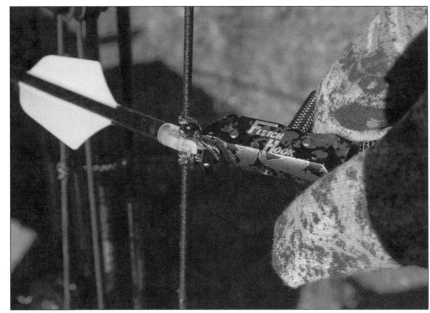

idea to shoot all these groups (5 total) twice or three times over just to make sure your group sizes don't deviate. When all is said and done, you compare all the groups you've shot and see which one is the best.

Some releases are more accurate than others, so it's important to test as many as possible.

No. 2:
Experiment with Releases

A good release-aid offers these features: high adjustability, low-torque head, and a smooth, smooth trigger.

Try different models to see which one offers that "crisp" trigger feel for improved shooting. Every brand will have a different feel. Releases with polished jaws tend to shoot the smoothest, as well, and greatly reduce bowstring or D-loop wear.

I favor wrist-strap releases with nylon-connecting straps as well, since they eliminate string torque and make adjustability even more precise. Models such as the Scott NCS Series, all Jim Fletcher models, Carter Quickie and One-Shot Series, Cobra Mamba Series, TRU-Fire Hurricane and Bulldog, T.R.U. Ball Cyclone or Short-N-Sweet, to name a few, have micro-adjustable nylon connectors.

The Carter Quickie 2 comes with a trigger adjustment system, where you can switch out tension springs for a lighter or heavier trigger pull.

Fact: Experimentation opens the door to better shooting.

No. 3:
Increasing Broadhead Performance

Shoot Different Broadheads: It's always wise to dabble with a few different broadhead models, and possibly even arrow shaft brands and fletching types. Also, if you often hunt in somewhat breezy conditions, shoot when the wind blows with different components and see which combination drifts the least amount. That's what you'll want to use when the hunt is on.

Use Maximum Fletching Helical: It's also a good idea to put your fletching on using maximum helical. "I think all vanes need to be fletched with a hard helical for hunting," says Mike

Today's rigid, compact fletching can increase front-of-center arrow weight and lessen wind drift. This tends to make them more accurate. Arizona Archery's Max Hunter vanes are a top choice.

TECH TIPS

Bow Sight Specs

Smaller sight pins mean less obscuring of the target at longer distances. The Sword Acu-Site offers pins sizes down to .010-inch, which takes aiming precision to a whole new level.

Do your best to choose a rugged yet very adjustable bow sight. For maximum accuracy, you'll want a sight with fairly small aiming beads and one with a precise bubble level.

Sight-Pin Specifications: For sight pins out to 40 or 50 yards, sight pin beads .029-inch are ideal. However, at farther distances, smaller micro-size beads allow for more aiming precision since they reduce target "block out." I prefer .019-inch beads if possible for long-range shooting.

Each pin also must be perfectly inline from one another. In other words, any "zigzag" pattern among pins will hurt horizontal accuracy. Though rare, some sights offer horizontal adjustability for each pin.

Second- and Third-Axis Leveling: This same sight should have a bubble level with third-axis capability. Nearly every bow sight has a second-axis bubble, which ensures you hold your bow level on relatively flat ground. Third-axis bubbling, however, accounts for the levelness of the bow when shooting up or downhill, which is a likely scenario in the mountains. Without this feature, you can easily miss shots despite a perfect aim and execution. Don't overlook it.

Sighting Plane: Some bow sights come with long extension bars. The premise behind this is simple: the longer the sight plane—the distance the sighting element is from your eye—generally speaking the more accurate and precise your aim becomes. Though extending the sight pins further away from your eye could induce a "shakier" sight picture, one who holds steady will be more accurate.

BY JOE BELL

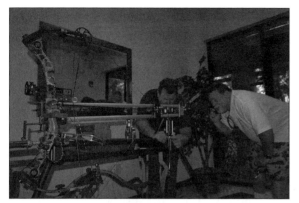

The author often uses a Hooter Shooter machine to determine what variables affect arrow accuracy.

Slinkard, pro shooter and owner of Winner's Choice Bowstrings. "This gives the arrow more spin and greater stability. This translates into improved accuracy."

Randy Ulmer also insists on strong helical. He uses very small fletching —AAE Plastifletch MAX measuring 2 inches long—on his hunting arrows, which are tipped with Rage or Rocky Mountain Snyper mechanical broadheads. With a Bitzenburger jig, he offsets the vanes to the strongest degree possible while still allowing proper adhesion. He uses an ultra-small-diameter Easton HIT-type shaft, mainly the Full Metal Jacket.

"A lot of bowhunters use store-bought arrows with vanes that are mounted either straight or only slightly offset," says Ulmer. "It's simply easier for manufacturers to glue them in place this way. However, you need a lot of helical on hunting arrows to get them spinning as quickly as possible, which allows for proper stabilization and maximum accuracy, especially with broadheads."

Shoot at Long-Range: According to Slinkard, shooting broadheads at long range will identify slight imperfections in your gear. "I shoot every arrow/broadhead combination at 70 yards," says Slinkard. "If the arrow will not hit within a 6-inch spot at this distance (after I am happy with my bow's tune) I will rotate or change the arrow nock. If that doesn't help, that arrow will not be with me on a big-game hunt. Most of the time you can tune inaccuracy out of a particular arrow, but not always."

Slinkard currently shoots a Tight Point Shuttle T-Lock 100 broadhead, though he's also fond of the Rocky Mountain Ti-100, which he has used for many years with exceptional results. "Both of these heads are ultra straight and I can shoot them in the same hole as my field points all the way out to 80 yards."

"I've done an extensive amount of shot testing in the wind using a shooting machine," says Ulmer. "Through this testing I've found the best arrow type, size broadhead and fletching for bucking the wind."

Arrow Spine: Proper arrow spine is crucial for good broadhead flight and penetration. Always err on the side of too stiff a spine rather than too weak. "Arrow spine selection is critical to getting your broadheads to fly like your field points," says Bob Mizek, chief engineer for New Archery Products. "I like and use the program from Archer's Advantage. This easy to use program covers all the popular brands, models, and sizes. It's found at www.archersadvantage.com.

Ulmer believes stiffer arrows tune better and shoot with greater forgiveness when using broadheads. He always uses one that's slightly stiff.

No. 4:
Arrow Speed

Many bowhunters prefer mechanical heads, since they tend to shoot similar to a field point inside 40 yards.

With fixed-blade broadheads, super-fast arrow speed will eventually cause some deterioration in shooting consistency. Every shooter will likely have a different "speed" threshold at which he can shoot fixed-blade heads with nearly the same degree of accuracy as field points. This is based largely on shooting form and just how fine-tuned the bow is. Group testing is the only way to determine this arrow speed limit.

Generally speaking, 270-to-280 fps seems to be the upper arrow speed limit for most shooters using fixed-blade broadheads of normal size. However, I do know of some guys who shoot around 300 fps and report excellent accuracy with compact fixed heads. It just all depends.

No. 5:
Altering FOC

Your arrow's Front of Center (FOC) weight can have a drastic accuracy affect. My suggestion is to shoot an FOC of 10 percent or more. This will "load" the tip so it can stay steady as it's subjected to intense air currents, particularly from wind blowing from the side. This increases arrow stability and obviously accuracy.

You can up FOC weight by using the lightest possible fletching that doesn't hinder proper drag for your arrow length and weight. Some bowhunters favor arrow wraps, or cresting. However, this feature adds additional rear-arrow weight, lowering the arrow's FOC weight, which I see as a major disadvantage.

Today's stiff, compact fletching, such as the Bohning Blazer and AAE Max Hunter, are lighter and therefore increase an arrow's FOC.

Fact: Never shoot an under-spined arrow; always err on the side of too stiff rather than not stiff enough.

No. 6:
Group Tune Arrows

Shooting arrow groups with different vanes and broadheads will tell you what groups the best.

Once your bow is offering a near bullet hole in paper, now's the moment of the true test. Roughly sight-in the bow and begin group testing at long-range. I prefer to shoot from about 50 yards and begin measuring my groups using both field points and broadheads. It's quite normal for your broadheads to group in a larger circle, but the circle shouldn't expand more than an inch or two.

Also, if these groups are spread out more than a couple inches from each other, I try to make a few micro-adjustments horizontally or vertically to the arrow rest until the groups come together. If accuracy suffers in any case, I return to the original tune and sight-in with broadheads. (*Note:* Always move the arrow rest in the direction of the field-point groups. For example, if your broadheads group to the left and high, move the arrow rest-arm to the right and slightly lower.)

Fact: Numbering your arrows will allow you to find those that are most accurate.

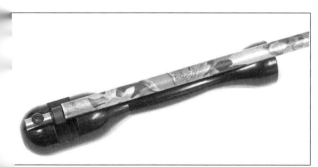

5's Arrow Squaring Device (ASD) is useful for achieving exact roadhead alignment.

Don't accept second-rate accuracy with fixed-blade heads. Try different models and you'll see some group quite well while others will not. Size of a head has some affect on tuning, but the broadhead's overall shape affects its aerodynamics. For high speed, consider heads like the G-5 Striker, Innerloc Stainless Extreme 100, Slick Trick 1-inch, Muzzy 100-grain 4-Blade, Rocky Mountain Blitz, NAP Nitron and Magnus Snuffer SS.

Bow Quivers: Do They Affect Accuracy?

After conducting two shooting-machine tests as well as one personal test, it appears a bow quiver could affect accuracy but *only slightly*. There's a slight point of impact change when removing as little as one arrow from the quiver (about 1 ounce), and less of a variance when removing a few more. At mid-range distances (40-to-45 yards), the impact change is not significant, particularly with a release-aid set-up, low-profile two-piece quiver, and compact fixed-blade heads. With mechanical heads, the point of impact change is really insignificant at these same distances.

With a fingers release, however, the impact change appears to be slightly more, possibly because of the intense arrow movement at release, which may magnify changes in bow weight. However, because of the difficulty in setting up a shooting machine with a fingers attachment, a shooting-machine test was not done.

One of the shooting tests was in a controlled indoors setting, using a shooting machine. These are the results. The test was done at 40 yards, and the bow set-up consisted of a Mathews Switchback (27-inch draw length, 68-pound pull), 26-inch Beman Elite Black Max arrows, Bohning Blazer vanes with maximum helical, 100-grain G5 Montec fixed-blade broadheads and Rocky Mountain Snyper expandable broadheads. Arrow speed: 265 fps. A low-profile 6-arrow bow quiver was used, starting with only 5 arrows in the quiver.

Arrow Group Impact—Averages

	From 5-to-4 Arrows in the Quiver	All Arrows Out
3 Arrow Groups Fixed-Blade Broadheads	1.6" left, .75" down	1.6" left, 1.5"down
3 Arrow Groups Snyper Mech. Broadheads	.5" down	Same

Points to note: During these tests, I noticed as arrows were drawn out, point of impact changes occurred to the left and low during one test. Whereas, during another test (although done outside with a very slight breeze present), arrows appeared to group slightly higher and higher as arrows were removed. A lot of this impact change is dependent on the type of quiver you use, where it's mounted on the bow and just how close it rides to the bow handle to minimize side-load.

The other test I performed a few years ago shooting my personal bow using a fingers release. The test was conducted outside on a calm morning. I shot three arrow groups at 45 yards using fixed-blade broadheads. I achieved only slightly better accuracy (about ½-inch better—really negligible) with the quiver off than with the quiver on, minus one arrow.

The point of impact change between five and four arrows in the quiver resulted in a change of about 1-½ inches to the right. As I removed more arrows from the quiver, the impact change was less and less significant. Remember this test included human error, so the results are not exact. Each arrow in the quiver weighed 425 grains.

During this test, I also made sure the bow weighed the same (7 pounds) by adding stabilizer/counter weights to ensure the same aiming and shot stability between the two set-ups.

Also, when group tuning, make sure to number each arrow and see if impact patterns develop. In many cases, the arrows you have chosen may not be uniform in spine and could drastically affect your accuracy tests. Try upper-tier, pre-sorted carbon arrows in this case, or switch to aluminum/carbon or all-aluminum shafts.

No. 7:
Nocks, Loops and Center Serving

D-Loop Set-Up: Don't ignore the D-shaped string loop; it offers more advantages than disadvantages. It's the secret to easy arrow tuning and more forgiveness.

With a string loop, fasten it to your string, and twist it up and down until you reach the point of perfect vertical arrow tuning. Once this is done, I like to "widen" the loop by serving in two 1/8-inch nocksets to surround the nock, or serve in one nockset below the nock. *(See Chapter 12 for details on serving tips and various styles of string loops.)*

TECH TIPS

Mass Bow Weight

I believe mass bow weight has some affect on how well a bow shoots, and this applies whether or not the archer demonstrates perfect shooting form. During these same quiver-accuracy tests, I noticed in a lot of cases that group sizes shrunk slightly when the weight of the quiver was added to the bow; this applied to both field points and broadheads. And this was while a shooting machine was holding the bow!

This reinforces something I've always thought: heavier bows seem to offer more shooting stability. They usually aim steadier, are more forgiving when torque is applied to the handle, and the overall mass of the bow simply moves less during the launching of the arrow, which leads to tighter groups and more consistent shooting. Don't just take my word for it; experiment on your own by adding counterweights and perhaps a heavier stabilizer to your bow. See what happens; I bet you'll shoot better.

This does two important things: It allows faster hook-ups to the string, since now the loop is larger. Secondly, it allows greater clearance now that the tail end of the arrow nock won't make contact with the loop when twist occurs. In some cases, this isn't necessary depending on your anchor style and release-aid.

Also, when serving a nockset only below the arrow nock, you're now pulling the bowstring back closer to the center of the bow. This places a degree of pressure of the arrow onto the arrow rest, which allows better tuning with some bows.

Nock Diameter and Center Serving Size: It's very important that your arrow nocks fit the bowstring's center serving properly; otherwise it will have some affect on accuracy.

Randy Ulmer maintains arrows nocks should fit fairly tight on the bowstring. "Basically, you want the serving to fill the nock's groove," he says. "You don't want any side to side movement when wiggling the arrow."

You must experiment with different diameter center serving material until you get the perfect fit with your chosen arrow nocks.

No. 8:
Bow Balance

To offset the weight of a bow-mounted quiver, Fuse makes the Sidekick stabilizer accessory.

A bow that tilts nastily forward at the shot is annoying, and can affect accuracy. A bow quiver, depending on the design, can really pull to one side, or create severe top heaviness. In either case, shooting consistency will suffer.

Target shooters know the importance of a well-balanced bow. When held up, their bows don't rock around from side to side. Instead, they hold perfectly plumb.

Of course, a hunting bow doesn't require the same diehard balancing act, but you should at least minimize this variable as much as you can, given that it doesn't take away from function in the field.

From left: Two-piece quivers that attach solidly and hug the bow's riser minimize side load and potential bow torque at the shot. The Fuse Posi-Lite, Fuse Caldera and Mathews Arrow Web are some of the best two-piece quivers on the market.

If you shoot with a bow quiver attached, don't put up with a lot of side torque. There are many great bow quivers on the market, but the best ones are solid two-piece designs that attach very close to the bow's riser. The closer it rides to the riser, the less it will rock the bow to the side, making it potentially more torque free and acccurate. Fuse and Mathews make excellent two-piece quivers that fit snug to the bow riser.

With one of my favorite Mathews bows, I use a short 3-inch Doinker Chubby Hunter stabilizer on the bowstring-side of the riser that effectively helps balance the bow. Even with a two-piece Mathews Arrow Web quiver attached and loaded with arrows, I recognize little side torque.

Fuse offers the Axium Sidekick stabilizer system that will offset the weight of any bow quiver on the market. It's a unique and effective accessory.

Also, recognize the importance of a stabilizer. A long design lends more accuracy to the bow, since it extends the bow's vertical plane and controls torque more effectively. But in some hunting situations, using a long stabilizer (12 inches long or so) is an inconvenience. Choose the longest model ideal for your specific style of hunting.

No. 9:
Peep Alignment

There are two schools of thought on aiming with a peep: align it with the bowsight's rounded pin guard, or simply center a specific sight pin in the peep. Both methods have pros and cons.

Aligning Peep with Guard: This method is perhaps the most popular today (obvious by the plethora of rounded bowsight housings available), since it allows the archer to maintain a consistent anchor point no matter what sight pin he uses. It also allows the use of a larger peep orifice, as

TECH TIPS

Exact Bow Sight-In

Use this two-step method to effectively sight-in your bow. The objective in this case is to adjust your sight pins first for horizontal and then for vertical accuracy.

To do this, use a strip of extra-thick colored tape and spread it vertically (up and down) across the target. Be sure to use a large strip, about 12-to-18 inches long. Now, stand back and shoot for the line, beginning first at 10 yards, then 20. Adjust your sight accordingly. Resist grouping the arrows in one spot along the line. The goal here is to group them anywhere along the line, or close to it. Simply let your sight pin "bob" along the line and focus on making a good shot. Once you feel confident of the adjustment, proceed with the vertical sight-in of each appropriate sight pin.

Perform the same as previously described, only this time remove the vertical line and make a horizontal one (left to right). Start shooting at the line from 20 yards using your 20-yard pin; adjust your sight accordingly. Then back up to further distances, sighting in the 30-, 40-, 50-yard pin and so on. This process could take two-to-three days, or longer, to obtain the most precise sight-in at long ranges. It's important not to rush the process; focus on executing a good shot each and every time.

Also, once your bow is sighted in using this method, be very cautious in making small adjustments as you shoot from one day to the next. Just because your arrows are hitting a couple inches one way today doesn't necessarily mean they'll do the same tomorrow. Slight form errors (an inconsistency in anchor or bow-hand position) could cause this, so keep this in mind. As a general rule, I don't alter my initial sight-in unless the impact change is drastically off or occurs repeatedly during the course of 2-to-3 practice sessions.

It's also common to notice a small point of impact change at the beginning of a practice session versus later on when your shooting muscles are warm and stretched. As a bowhunter, your first arrow is often the most important one, so sight-in the bow when your shooting muscles are more on the colder side.

Some experts prefer to center each individual sight pin in the peep sight, while others prefer to align the sight's circular pin guard with the peep sight for positive aiming alignment. Both methods work well.

well, increasing low-light visibility. The downside in this method, I believe, is how it takes a few seconds longer to acquire your target. It's a three-step process: align peep with guard, find the sight pin you need and aim.

Centering Pin with Peep: I've tried both methods and I seem to favor this one. It's more natural for my eye to center the pin in the peep. That being the case, I can get on target with lightning speed since two steps are involved—center peep with pin and aim. The downside is that as I shoot longer-range pins, I have to nudge my nose upward to obtain the correct alignment with the peep and pin. However, I anchor in such a way along my jawbone that it doesn't seem to affect my accuracy.

I'm no pro shooter, so I asked my friend Mike Slinkard how he does it. He says he prefers to align the peep to the sight housing, but believes either method allows for the same degree of accuracy. He just likes the idea of using a larger peep sight.

Randy Ulmer, on the other hand, prefers to center the pin in the peep. "Your eye will naturally center the pin you are using in the peep," he says. "I set up my peep height so my 20-yard pin is positioned at a point where if I lowered the peep anymore I'd feel uncomfortable. With this setting, I am comfortable using my bottom pin."

Darin Cooper also told me he centers the pin in the peep as well.

He has three separate reasons for using this method.

1. Your subconscious tends to center an object you're looking at through the peep, so if you're focusing on your target behind the 20-yard pin at the top of a circular pin housing, chances are you'll tend to drift away from centering the housing toward centering the pin. This is especially true if you're forced to hold for an extended period. If I start with the pin centered I tend to stay centered on it.

2. I also prefer to use a peep (approx. 3/32-inch) that is somewhat smaller than most sight housings at full draw. I have found that my accuracy improves at longer range with this size aperture, but it makes it impossible to center most sight housings.

3. I use Archer's Advantage **www.archersadvantage.com** software to set my pin gaps. This works extremely accurately when you center each pin the same way that you would center a small target scope on a moveable target sight as you adjust it for each yardage. If you center the housing your pin gaps will not calculate properly. Using Archer's Advantage to set my pins and print a tape for my Sure-Loc Lethal Weapon Max provides me with the ultimate in accuracy and is a huge time saver when I'm forced to set up a new prototype at the last minute," explains Cooper.

Peep size all depends on your aiming style, anchor position and bow length. For basic release bows (32-to-37 inches axle to axle), I prefer a 3/16-inch Fletcher Tru-Peep. Those who align the pin with the sight housing may need a larger peep, such as the Tru-Peep Max Hunter (1/4-inch orifice) to visibly see the outer ring of the sight. *(Note:* When using this method, it's vital that you place the complete outer ring of the sight's guard in the inner portion of your peep. The sight guard shouldn't be blurry.)

> ## TECH TIPS
>
> ## Fletching Perfection
>
> Consistency is the name of the game in every aspect of archery. For this reason, when building arrows keep everything the same. Obviously this means using the same shaft length, color fletching, inserts, nocks, and glue. However, it also means using the same exact fletching jig to assemble and repair every one of your arrows. Every brand of jig, despite constant adjusting, seems to mount fletching in a slightly different orientation. This could affect arrow speed and point of impact from one arrow to the next. This is being a bit nitpicky, but the accuracy gain could be well worth it.

Ulmer prefers the smallest peep possible, but one that allows suitable light allowance in hunting situations. "Your focal length is much longer with a small peep. This allows you to more easily focus on the pin and the target at the same time, making for a more accurate shot," he says. "If I hunted Alaska, Oregon or another dark woods region, I'd use a little larger peep, but most of my hunting is in the mountain West where it's always pretty bright out when shooting."

No. 10:
Use a Different Bow Grip

A narrow bow grip has less surface area, which makes it harder to grip the bow wrong, or to torque it during the shot. For this reason, it increases accuracy.

Something as small as the bow grip can have a significant affect on shooting accuracy. I've found bows with slender throats shoot the most consistently day in, day out.

According to Ulmer, the wider the grip the more likely you are to torque it from left to right.

With this kind of riser-metal grip, many shooters like wrapping it with hockey tape to warm it. However, Ulmer warns against this. "I don't recommend doing that," he says. "The more friction you have on the handle the easier it is to torque the grip. The bow should settle into your hand and not need friction to

Cavalier's Avalanche arrow rest is a super-accurate design. It comes with a functional, quiet arrow holder as well (right).

Fuse's String StealthShot not only deadens bowstring noise but it keeps the bowstring from oscillating past the brace-height position. This alleviates string slap for a more accurate and forgiving set-up.

keep the grip from slipping. If it's slipping out to your thumb, then the handle is not properly placed in your hand."

Mike Slinkard not only uses a narrow, riser-type grip, but he actually places a small stud on the bottom/rear of the grip to accentuate consistency. "I do this in the area where I want the pressure to be concentrated in my hand," said Slinkard. "This stud does not cause any pain in the hand; it just serves as an unmistakable location of the grip in my hand. I have found that this greatly increases my accuracy and consistency, especially in hunting situations where you may be in an odd position, cold, or otherwise distracted."

The process of super tuning your bow can be time consuming. However, this time will prove very beneficial once your arrow groups begin to shrink more and more. Do the work and you'll enter a new level of accuracy.

Section 2

Pro-Level Shooting Technique

Chapter 7
Expert Shot Execution

The Pros Tell How It's Done

"A failure establishes only this, that our determination to succeed was not strong enough."
—*John Christian Bovee*

When using back-tension to trigger the shot, your mind has an easier time focusing on aiming and leaving the actual release up to the subconscious mind. This creates a surprise release and alleviates you from target panic.

What defines a perfect shot? The arrow that drills the bull's-eye, or the 10-ring on the 3-D target, or the spot just behind a deer's shoulder, is proof positive that we did it right. Yes, we all agree that arrows that find their mark mean a lot. But over the long haul, consistent arrow accuracy doesn't just come this way.

According to every archery coach or pro archer with whom I've spoken, a shot must "feel" right to be a good one. Once an archer can define that perfect sensation during the shot process, and he does all he can to repeat it, you might be surprised to find out that a good-feeling shot eventually becomes a perfect, in-the-10 or in-the-vitals shot, nearly every time.

There is an incredible upside to shooting this way: Your internal energy is all hinged on proper shooting form, and *not* the results, which can easily vary from day to day if your technique is not consistent. Keeping your technique "results" focused is a poor way to approach shooting, and will eventually force you into a slump, or degrade your confidence severely. Good days become very good, and bad days very bad. And, as you well know, confidence is extremely necessary in performing well in the clutch. When your primary focus is on form, consistency almost always follows. That's what expert-level bow shooting is all about.

TECH TIPS

Back-Tension, Darin Cooper's 8 Steps to Success

Darin Cooper relies on executing the shot using his back muscles, whether he's shooting a pro-level target match or making an important shot on a trophy-class animal, such as this big Idaho bull.

Here is a step-by-step process that you can use to execute a back-tension shot:

1. Draw the bow to full draw without fully engaging your anchor point.
2. Pre-load the shot (gently pull past the valley and into the back wall of the cam).
3. Find your anchor point while maintaining tension on the back wall.
4. Center the aiming pin in the peep-sight and visually acquire the target.
5. Stare at the center of the target and ease the pin down to it.
6. Hook the finger or thumb around the trigger and tension it to 90 percent.
7. Gradually increase drawing pressure into the back wall of the cam by contracting the back muscles. Visualize moving the drawing elbow straight back behind the arrow until the shot fires.
8. Follow through.

In Chapter 1, I mentioned the fundamentals of good shooting form. In this chapter, we'll take it one step further by outlining the finer details of shot technique. Here you will find how the pros approach shooting, specifically with a release-aid. *(Chapter 8 discusses the fingers release in detail.)*

This sequence shows proper execution using a dynamic release. Note the explosion after the release, indicating the use of back tension.

Shoot Using Your Back

This is what separates ordinary shooters from great ones, or at least the ones that shoot very well under pressure. Instead of letting just a single finger (the one on the trigger) *control* when the release fires—a lot of pressure on just one little body part—the pros allow the very large muscles in the back to make it happen. This is called the "dynamic" release, or a process the pros refer to as "back tension."

"The actual release should be totally subconscious," says Mike Slinkard. "By this I mean the conscious mind must be totally immersed in aiming, leaving the much more powerful subconscious mind to trigger the release through back tension."

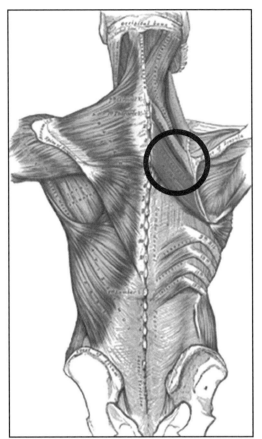

This illustration shows the location of the back muscles you should use to execute the shot.

To carry out a dynamic release, you must use your rhomboid muscles, which are the large muscles closest to your spine. You do this simply by squeezing the shoulder blades toward each other. There are two ways to do this, either by pulling with your draw-side back muscles, or by pulling with both sides of your back.

"I use the draw-side back muscles to control aiming and to release the shot," says Randy Ulmer. "I believe that no aiming or control of the bow should come from the left arm or shoulder (right-handed archer). I like to think of the left side of my body as inanimate—something I have no control over. My left arm is a post and I can't exert any control with my left hand. If I need to aim left or right, I must do so with my right side, which is being controlled with the powerful muscles close to my spine. My left arm only moves as my torso moves."

Scott Shultz, president of Robinson Labs, past-pro-level shooter, and expert bowhunter, describes back-tension as a feeling of "pressure" building up in your back rather than the actual physical movement rearward of your arm.

"I often explain it like this: If the letoff weight of your bow at full draw is 18 pounds, then as you settle into the spot with your sight pin, you then apply back tension, bringing the tension to 19 pounds. Then, when the shot goes off, you should be pulling maybe 20 pounds of tension," Shultz says. "With the solid back wall of most eccentrics today, these extra pounds of pull don't really continue to draw, or overdraw, the bow. This extra tension produces a good strong release every time."

Unlike Shultz and Ulmer, Slinkard prefers to tighten his back muscles abruptly upon full draw and reaching his anchor point, which seems to help stabilize his aim and gives his mind nothing to worry about but to *aim...aim...aim*. His finger works the trigger subconsciously. He never thinks about it—it just happens. Regardless of the method, when done right, both methods will instill a surprise release, promoting consistency.

To learn this process of pulling the trigger using your back muscles, shoot up close into a target, with your eyes shut, hundreds of times until the process becomes totally automatic. It could take several weeks, even months, of blind-bale practice to store the technique in your subconscious and allow the body's muscle memory to take over. From that point onward, it's important to trust the process. Don't think about it during practice, only when you shoot up close with your eyes closed.

Fact: True accuracy comes from using a surprise release.

With a strap-on release, use your finger to form a "hook," then squeeze your back muscles together. This will effectively tug the trigger rearward, rather than triggering the shot with the flex of your fingertip.

To perform this process using a wrist-strap release, adjust it so the trigger rides pretty deep along your index finger, anywhere between the first and second creases. Next, form a "hook" along the trigger using your finger, applying light pressure. (With plenty of practice and by adjusting your release, you'll get a sense of the right amount of load to place on the trigger initially; set your trigger's tension light but not too light to begin with.)

Then start your "motor" by activating those back muscles until the forearm, hand and finger-hook are moving. Simply maintain the tension until—surprise—the shot is gone. To do it right, you can't think about it at all. Stay focused on aiming, nothing more.

With a T-handle thumb-release, you simply get a firm hold on the release with the base of your thumb firmly planted against the contour of the release. As you apply back tension, the release handle will naturally pivot toward your thumb, forcing it into the trigger. You shoot a back-tension release (one without a trigger–Carter Colby, Scott Longhorn, TRU Ball Sweet Spot, etc.) the same way until it fires automatically.

"The only way I have found to effectively train the subconscious is through very simple repetition," says Slinkard. "By concentrating on one micro aspect of the shot sequence at a time until it happens automatically without conscious thought, each and every time (like turning the wheel of your car when you reach a bend in the road)."

Why Not Command the Release?

Some great archers insist on using a "static" release, which is performed by pressing the trigger once the sight pin settles on the spot. The mind simply registers "now!" and the shot is off. That's basically how everyone who doesn't receive expert coaching shoots a bow

Mental Pre-Shot Checklist

When rehearsing the perfect shot on a blind bale, be sure you follow a specific shot sequence. How you arrange your list isn't so important, but what *is* important is that you follow it during practice sessions *exactly* in order, *each and every time*.

My shot checklist goes like this: 1. Nock arrow. 2. Set foot position (stance). 3. Hook up release. 4. Set bow hand position. 5. Raise bow to level position. 6. Apply tension on bowstring; set "pressure point" on bow grip to hand. 7. Draw bow (slowly and without raising bow much, if any) while inhaling a deep breath. 8. Find my anchor. 9. Glide sight pin up on target. 10. Exhale a half-breath. 11. Begin pulling with my back. 12. Jump into aiming mode—shot breaks in about 4 seconds. 13. Keep your arm up. 14. Check to make sure your hand lightly brushes your ear.

to begin with. I should point out that some expert archers actually prefer this shooting method—they believe it's more accurate since the pin doesn't have time to float too much on target. However, most archers are better off using a true surprise release since it breeds more consistency with most personality types.

In a nutshell, there are downsides to shooting on command. The first problem is knowing when the release will fire—a mental trigger that eventually leads to anticipation. After hundreds and hundreds of shots, the mind will pick up on the timing of the release, and as it does so, it will rebel. Involuntary responses such as flinching and punching the trigger start to happen. After time, you're basically just forcing the shot as soon as the sight pin even touches the bull's-eye. Relaxation at the shot is now gone, and accuracy will suffer.

Fact: There are more disadvantages than advantages to commanding the release.

Pro shooter John Dudley illustrates a comfortable, consistent anchor.

Another key problem with commanding the release is the lack of back tension involved in using the technique. It's important to create rearward tension constantly on the bowstring to maintain a consistent draw length and a cleaner release.

And, finally, the muscles in your back are much stronger than the muscles in your arms and shoulders, which are the muscles mainly used when commanding the trigger. Because of this, applying back-tension at full draw allows for a steadier hold and aim, and allows you to hold the bow at full draw for extended periods of time with less fatigue (useful in hunting situations).

Establish a Consistent Anchor

For a solid anchor, use the web of your hand to cradle your cheekbone as shown here.

"With regard to anchor points, the one thing I notice shooters doing a lot is pulling the bowstring into their face much too hard," says Slinkard. "The string should come *lightly* in contact with the tip of the nose and not past it, nor should it come in hard against the side of your face or jaw area. Those that anchor too hard tend to have left and right accuracy problems."

Scott Shultz considers the anchor point the most critical part of consistent shooting. "I prefer to look at the anchor as a byproduct of perfect draw length, good shooting form, and a well adjusted peep," says Shultz. "If you must wiggle and scrunch around to settle in a position to see through the peep, something is wrong. A good anchor is comfortable above all else, which will make it more consistent."

Aiming

It's a simple concept, but many archers make it complicated. The object is to ease the sight pin on the target, relax and allow the natural motion of movement to occur until the shot breaks. No one can hold the sight pin perfectly steady, particularly at longer distances, and fighting it only induces problems.

Some archers prefer to follow an aiming pattern, by drawing out an imaginary "8" on the bull's-eye or encircling it over and over using the sight pin. Others prefer to simply let it do whatever it wants to do as they focus only on where they want to hit.

I prefer a different method, particularly for long-range shooting. I like to imagine I'm holding a telescoping pole, and I'm trying to drive the eye of it through the center of the target. To do so, I know I must hold the pin fairly steady on target to place the pole in the bull's-eye. I envision the pole moving ever so slowly outward…and I must wait, and aim, while it hits. This alleviates my mind from thinking about the release, which then just happens subconsciously after about 3-to-4 seconds of thinking about all this.

"You must convince your mind that sight movement is natural," says Tim Strickland, past Olympic archery coach, certified NFAA coach, past pro-level shooter and expert bowhunter. "Besides, your mind and body have a way of correcting through motion to make sure the arrow finds the spot. In fact, the more you resist sight motion, the less chance you have of consistently hitting what you're shooting at."

As discussed in Chapter 1, there are two ways to aim—you can focus on the target and blur the pin, or blur the target and focus on the pin. Both methods work.

"So many archers address the target, or animal, at full draw with the sight pin slowly, slowly dropping or rising toward the desired spot," says Shultz. "But I believe you should never, ever, aim at the target or animal while the bow arm slowly moves the sight pin toward the spot. I believe the sight pin shouldn't be recognized, even considered or validated as in existence, until it is located on the target or on the animal.

An accurate bowhunter becomes immersed in the aiming process, allowing the subconscious mind and muscle memory to trigger the shot. You simply aim and wait until the arrow fires.

"What I mean is that when the archer begins the shot, he should immediately place the pin exactly where it should be. Then, and only then, should the settling in and aiming part of the process begin," Shultz continues. "This requires a lot of thought and discipline, but it assures that when the release goes off, whenever that is, the arrow goes where you want it."

Fact: No archer can hold the sight pin perfectly steady, so don't try.

Also, make sure you smoothly come up to target and use your body to correct the sight picture, not your bow arm. This increases steadiness.

TECH TIPS

Muscle Memory

Muscle memory is the most important component in shooting correctly, and allows you to ingrain what a perfect shot feels like. In the beginning, it will take months of repetitive close-range shooting (with eyes closed) to establish the muscle memory required to shoot using back-tension. Once this process is totally committed to the subconscious, it becomes automatic through the act of muscle memory. From here, you can keep your focus on one thing only—aiming.

Once back-tension and a surprise release becomes part of your shooting, you should still occasionally practice close-range, blind-bale shooting just to reinforce this habit. It's wise to shoot 5-to-10 arrows at a close-range butt (with eyes closed) before you start any practice session. Also, closing out the practice with several shots at 15 or 20 yards will reinforce good muscle memory and additional shooting confidence.

When you have time, take it one step further and have blank-bale-only practice days, where the only arrows you shoot for that day are with your eyes closed. Trust me, this will payoff big time when the pressure is seemingly unbearable.

The key to pro-level shooting is to master proper technique and go on autopilot. Train your body right, by the act of repetitive muscle memory, and success will follow.

Reducing Your Range of Motion

Range of motion is essentially how much your sight moves as you aim at the spot. The degree of movement will have some bearing on accuracy when using a surprise release. Simply put, when using good form, the less you move on target, the more accurate you'll be. In other words, if your sight pin rolls around in a 2-inch circle, theoretically, you'll shoot 2-inch arrow groups for that day.

Establish a consistent breathing program while you shoot. The author likes to inhale a full breath as he draws the bow. Once he reaches full draw, he aligns his peep so it centers the aiming pin, then exhales, letting about half the air out. Then he focuses on aiming. When coming up with a consistent breathing routine, be sure to train yourself to release the arrow within 8 seconds from the time you draw back to when the arrow fires. This will prevent you from losing strength and your ability to concentrate.

To reduce range of motion, you'll have to spend a great deal of time experimenting. "Things like bow balance, stabilizer configuration, draw length, bow poundage and effective let off are all important in establishing a bow that will hold better," says Slinkard. "However, I think the most important variables are the type of grip on the bow one uses and the use of back-tension.

"I have found that the best grip for most shooters (and the one most champions seem to use) is the low-wrist grip. The idea is to put the brunt of the pressure from the handle as close to the straight-line position with the bones on the arm as possible. This alleviates muscle involvement in the hand, which destroys holding ability."

Notes on Breathing

Experts believe one's breathing routine will affect shooting ability. The best routine will vary from one archer to the next. However, regardless of how you do it, again, it must remain consistent on each shot.

The best advice here is to establish a rhythm where you may take a deep breath in during the draw, settle in to anchor, then let out some air before finalizing the shot. Experiment and see what makes you feel most comfortable and steady on target.

Visualizing the perfect shot can go a long way to actually making one.

"If you take a deep breath of air, your body naturally becomes tense, resulting in a less stable hold," says Slinkard. "This is why I like to let out three-fourths of the air in my lungs when aiming. This seems to yield the best hold for me."

"I exhale as I draw the bow, take a full breath as I pre-load into the wall anchor and get the trigger pre-loaded," says Darin Cooper. "I hold my breath as I start to aim."

Visualization

Just imagining something can go a long way in achieving it. This is called positive affirmation through the art of visualization. Some of the world's best athletes in all venues use visualization to increase performance. It's simple to do, too.

Paint a positive mental image in your mind before you come to full draw. Picture everything, from right down to how you clip the release to the string, to how you set your bow hand, to

TECH TIPS

Triggerless Release: Pure Magic

The best way to beat habitual trigger punching is to switch to a release that has no trigger. With this kind of release, it's impossible to "time" the shot the moment the sight pin is on target. Instead, you wait for the shot to break as the sight pin does what it's supposed to—move in and around the spot until the shot just goes. It promotes a true surprise release. This is why nearly all the pros shoot one during the off-season or for target or 3-D tournament use. This tool, when used right, really puts the snuff on target panic.

I will warn you, however, these releases take some time to master. The key is to shoot it up close for the first 50 shots or so, then ease back to 10 yards, then 20, and so on. In no time you'll get a feel for it. During the first few shots, it will seem like forever to release the arrow. This is good. It will force your conscious mind to do what you want it to do instead of messing up the shot—that is, to aim and nothing else.

Triggerless releases are not designed for hunting, but I would suggest using one if you have a bad case of target panic. It's better to blow a shot opportunity because of a slow-release time than to wound an animal. The best model I've used for hunting is the TRU Ball Sweet Spot 4. The Carter Solution is my second favorite (slower to load/reload but it seems more accurate). Make either one hunt-ready by "warming" it using athletic tape and applying a wrist cord so you can keep it close at hand.

After you shoot, monitor the position of the bow. When you use back tension, the bow will push out a bit and to the left and your hand will end up behind your head somewhere.

the draw, to centering the peep, to looking at the sight pin. Think about how you breathe and when. Most importantly, think about just letting the pin float on the spot, while you use your back muscles to trigger the shot.

I've never met an archer who tried visualization techniques and felt displeased with the results. It works.

"Using imagery can tap the subconscious and instill proper thinking," says Strickland. "A great example of a very successful athlete using imagery is Jack Nicklaus. He always imagines the line the ball needs to take and sees the ball go in the hole, every time, before he ever steps up to putt."

"When I first started using imagery, I would stand in front of a mirror and mimic a shot so I could feel and see what I was doing at the same time," said Strickland. "Doing this helped me get my shot and follow-through consistent. The nice thing is your subconscious cannot tell the difference between actual and imagined instances, and you can practice this anywhere."

Aim Time

Every archer will have a comfort zone as to how long he can hold at full draw without beginning to tire. Ideally, you always want to shoot before your mind and muscles begin to weaken. So in a sense, you can actually aim/hold for too long.

"My shot will usually go in about 5 seconds from the time I get steady and on target," Slinkard says. "Anything over about 8 seconds and I must either let down or start the aiming process over with a new breath."

For Shultz, he says he routinely holds up to 11 seconds in a target-shooting environment when using a target-type triggerless release, but for hunting he doesn't hold as long.

Fact: Resist aiming for longer than 8 seconds for optimum results.

"If my shot isn't gone in 7-to-8 seconds, I'll let it down," says Cooper. "Five-to-7 seconds is a good goal for executing the shot once you hold your breath because your visual acuity will start to decrease rapidly after 7 seconds. More training and better fitness will allow you

BY JOE BELL

How To Beat Target Panic: 10 Helpful Fixes

Target panic is archery's worst illness, but it can be beat, despite what some believe. Many psychological problems seem complicated, but, in truth, are rather simple and can be remedied. Here are some simple facts and fixes that will place you on the road to success as you overcome this mood-altering, accuracy-destroying archery problem.

First off, target panic is nothing to be ashamed of...most archers get it at some point. It's not a personal weakness...it's simply a mental development that occurs when your shooting style becomes overly complicated. Serious, passionate archers are most prone to getting panic. Why? Because they shoot a lot.

Target panic is not something you can suddenly eliminate. You develop it slowly, so you must learn to control it slowly. In other words, you have to shoot through it. Implementing discipline and smart practice techniques are the only ways to overcome or at least minimize panic.

Fix No. 1:
Establish a Comfortable Shot

Shoot hundreds and hundreds of shots with your eyes closed, which will help to establish a new release technique and a new feeling of shot calmness. Do this for at least three weeks.

The trick to good shooting is to listen to your mind and body. Shoot only when you feel energized and totally alert, otherwise you'll refuel bad habits and technique. Don't ever rush the shooting process, and don't ever shoot when you feel physically weak. Good archery is all about discipline. Tell yourself shooting is only useful when you're relaxed and in control. Don't ever get into a mode where you feel the need to shoot a certain number of arrows. Shoot only as many as you can with 100-percent full concentration.

Fix No. 2:
Shoot a lot at 10 or 15 Yards

Shooting at a large 10 or 15-yard target can work wonders. Any archer will feel comfortable at this range, without freezing or feeling less in control. Blind-bale shooting alone won't allow you to overcome panic; it's particularly useful in establishing repetitive form, which will enhance accuracy. The target is what causes the panic, so you need to learn to control your emotions with the target in front of you.

With enough practice at this distance, an archer will feel what a relaxed shot is all about. Also, try shooting multiple pins at close range—in other words, you can aim with your 40- or 60-yard pin at a large 15-yard butt. With target panic, you want to eliminate any surprises, and practicing all day at close range using only your top pin, then backing up to 40 yards can send any archer back to a state of shooting anxiety once again. By instead sticking to close range, an archer can become fully aware of what it's like to track along the target with these "other pins" and hopefully aim solidly.

Fix No. 3:
Be Machine-Like

How you practice has a huge affect on shooting control. Always work at your shooting drills systematically. This means working through the process like a machine, never skipping a step in the shooting process. This is not fun, but your subconscious mind (what you use to shoot with) is only programmed properly through direct commands delivered over and over again. If you change these commands by altering steps in the shooting process, it will quickly become confused and won't know how to process a good shot when the pressure is on.

Why do you think beginners never get target panic? Because they approach shooting with an ordered mind—draw, anchor, aim, release. They don't know enough to confuse their subconscious. But as they begin to learn more and more about shooting, they begin to change things, eventually confusing their minds and complicating the shot process. And with improper practice techniques, this is when target panic hits.

Fix No. 4:
Forget the Bad Shots

Build positive reinforcement, not negative. Every athlete, and archer will perform less than expected. Let bad feelings go and focus on form—nothing else. Base your shooting on what feels good, not what looks bad.

Fix No. 5:
Use a Surprise Release

Insist on using your back muscles to trigger the shot, subconsciously of course. This is the most foolproof method to overcome shot anticipation, which is a form of panic.

continued on next page...

Fix No. 6:
Ignore Sight Movement–Just Shoot the Shot

Tell yourself a moving sight pin is normal and is acceptable as you focus on the target. Trust your shot training and ignore sight movement. Know that a sight pin out of the spot can still mean a dead-center hit!

Fix No. 7:
Establish a Pre-Release Cue

Ignore the visual cue to shoot with all your might!! Tell yourself you absolutely cannot shoot unless you perform some kind of a bodily motion, such as loading up your back muscles, moving your elbow rearward, or simply feeling your hand and bow arm muscles completely relax.

Fix No. 8:
Shoot a Triggerless Release

Try this kind of a release for a while. It will force long-term aiming, instead of encouraging you to pull the trigger the moment the sight pin crosses the target. Many experts suggest doing all your off-season shooting with a triggerless release.

Fix No. 9:
Use an Ultra-Deep Fingers Release

If you shoot with fingers and often freeze up before placing your sight pin on the bull's eye or an animal's chest, grip the bowstring ultra deep—in the second, upper crease on your fingers—by nearly bending your fingers into the edge of your palm. You'll feel more secure and stronger at not letting go now.

From here, slowly bring your sight pin on target, and let it settle for a couple to a few seconds (make sure you aren't shooting too much weight), then as you relax, withdraw your fingers and let the bowstring gradually roll into the first crease. Perform back-tension, and simply relax the back of your hand to free the bowstring. Save this technique as a last resort.

Fix No. 10:
Get a Coach

The best medicine for fighting target panic is to enlist the help of a qualified archery coach. He is well equipped to help you tackle this crippling disease.

a slightly longer window. Under certain hunting conditions, I'll double pump the shot. If I'm forced to stay at full draw I'll exhale and take another breath or multiple breaths so my system can recover until the shot develops. When it's time, I quickly inhale and pull through the shot."

Identifying Proper Follow-Through

According to Strickland, when you demonstrate proper back-tension, then once the shot breaks your bow arm should naturally move slightly out and to the left (from the tension in your bow hand and the thrust of the bow), and your release hand should move rearward. Even though the arrow is gone, your body must remain active, with your muscles still continuing that same "motion" as they had been doing during the shot.

While this is happening, you need to keep your attention on the aiming spot, until the arrow hits. That defines proper follow-through.

When you place a high emphasis on shooting the arrow properly rather than measuring the outcome of the shot by the arrow's impact, what you'll find is that hitting your mark becomes repetitively easier. This, in turn, makes you a more accurate archer.

BY JOE BELL

Chapter 8
Revitalizing the Fingers Release

Techniques for Awesome Accuracy

"Continuous effort, not strength or intelligence, is the key to unlocking our potential."
—Liane Cardes

Coupled with the right equipment and set-up, a well-practiced fingers shooter can deliver superb accuracy.

Who said you couldn't achieve hair-splitting accuracy with fingers? The truth is, you can. Here's some of the best advice out there for making a smooth, deadly shot using fingers.

Grip the String Right

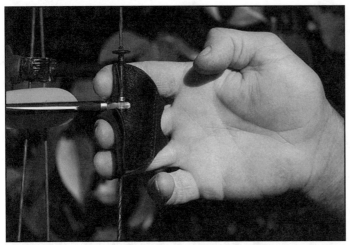

One important variable in maintaining excellent accuracy with fingers is to ensure your shooting hand remains straight throughout the draw. This will minimize string torque, which can degrade shooting consistency.

This is where shooting consistency comes into play. Two goals are involved with releasing the bowstring well with fingers. **1.** Keep as little contact as possible with the bowstring, while maintaining a level of control and comfort. **2.** Ensure the fingers stay limp, relaxed, and torque-free as they slip out of the way of the bowstring at the moment of the release.

To accomplish this, make a fairly deep "hook" on the bowstring using two or three fingers and make sure the back of your hand remains straight from the time of draw to full anchor. If the hand is not straight, horizontal string torque will occur, increasing side-to-side movement of the string (and arrow), potentially ruining accuracy. This is perhaps the No. 1 form flaw in shooting with fingers.

Once at full draw, depending on the degree of angle in the string and finger pinch, adjust your finger pressure accordingly. Some archers like to release almost all string pressure off the top or bottom finger, dragging it on the string, so to speak. When this happens, essentially the release is done with only two fingers (with various degrees of pressure on the top or bottom finger). Some will even drop the top or bottom finger off the string completely. You should experiment to see which version offers you the greatest control as well as the best accuracy.

Fact: The back of the hand must remain straight for a smooth, torque-free fingers shot.

As a long-time fingers shooter, I've tried a variety of techniques, including dropping the bottom finger entirely, but accuracy didn't change much for me when I did and dropping this finger seemed to slow my anchor/shot time down some.

Fingers-Shooting Insights

The author insists on shooting bows with gentle valleys and a hard wall when using a fingers release.

Adams believes fingers help him make tough, quick shots, which seem ever present in the field. His success speaks for itself.

Release: "When I release, I don't pull my hand back," says Nogara. "I kind of have a dead release, but I use back-tension. Once the arrow goes, I'm totally relaxed. The bow just slowly rocks forward. When you're shooting longer distances, you are actually holding better form at 70 yards because your follow through is more visible. As I'm watching the arrow through the sight guard, I'm more aware of my form, my follow through."

showing only the footprint of my broadhead, nothing else."

I have a patent on this tuning method—Weight Compensation Tuning Method. It's the most precise tuning method I've ever used."

Back-tension: "I go down on target with my sight, this way I'm not using my deltoid muscles to raise up," shares Nogara. "My back is in motion first, then I start to come down, and when my pin is on target, I level my bubble—then the shooting process starts from there."

Anchor: "I lock in pretty hard," says Adams. "I place the index finger in the corner of my mouth, and I have full pressure on all sides of my hand against my face/jaw. The string clears my nose just by a little bit—about 1/8-inch."

Choose a good tab, such as this Neet Comfort Tab, which has an ultra-durable, ultra-slick leather face.

Tabs: "I use a homemade tab modification of the time tested cant-pinch calf hair tab-made out of a single layer of Chap leather," says Adams. "I use the smooth side of the leather against the string and the rough side on my fingers. It doesn't shrink when it gets wet and it lasts a long time. I can usually get five years of use from it before needing a new one."

Tuning: "I spend a lot of time tuning and want a perfect paper tear with a broadhead," says Adams. "I don't tune with fletching, with and without a broadhead. I replace the 54 grains of fletching with 54 grains of electrician's tape wrapped around the shaft. The projectile has the same weight this way.

"I start shooting this 'bare' shaft at point blank range (3 feet) then move back to 6-to-10 feet, and finish shooting it at about 30 feet. I want a perfect slit in the paper,

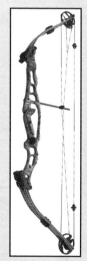 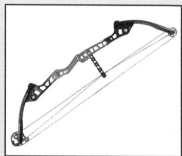

Hoyt's Montega and Mathews' Apex are longer, smoother, more forgiving bows well suited for fingers shooting.

"I don't push in against the side of my face at all," says Huffman. "In fact, the tip of my nose barely touches the string. I use my thumb and web of my hand to create a 'V' which

Finger-Shooting Insights, continued...

Angelo Nogara with a great Nevada mule deer.

locks in against my jawbone, which provides a consistent anchor."

Aim Time: "If I hold more than about 8 seconds, the shot isn't going to be good," says Nogara. "If I hold longer, weird things happen. The shoulder starts coming out of its low and locked position. I take a breath, go to full draw, then as I'm locked in and aiming, I let out a half-breath, then everything relaxes. Then the shot is off."

Bows: "I experimented down to 36 inches with fingers," says Adams. "My benchmark is to shoot an Indoor 300 Round. Right now I'm shooting a 280-to-290 score. Years ago, I did a lot of experimenting shooting this indoor round with bows of different lengths. For every inch shorter the bow is, I'll miss another three arrows. It's a progression, the more finger pinch I get the less smooth of a release I achieve. There's a smooth line of accuracy degradation as you shorten the bow.

"I shoot around a 9-inch brace height, 46-inch axle-to-axle bow. The other forgiveness factor is the more letoff on the bow, the poorer I shoot. I shoot 50 percent right now. With 60 percent I don't get as good accuracy, and at 65 I get even poorer accuracy.

"I use a Reflex Caribou Wheel & ½. My model has a special round-wheel-draw-cycle feel with a long valley. I need a long valley since I creep ahead close to ½-inch before I let go."

"Mathews Apex is the bow I shoot," says Huffman. "I think it's the best fingers bow out there. I can get by with a 38-to-39-inch-axle length, but you have to be careful. To me the Conquest is less forgiving. I shoot a 28-inch draw, 60 pounds."

"I use a Mathews Conquest 3, with the Super Soft Cam and 60-percent letoff," says Nogara. "This cam has a longer valley and no hard wall. It's set at 72 pounds,

using Easton ACC 3-60 arrows. For target tournament shooting, I use a Conquest 3 set at 59 pounds, and Easton X10 arrows. I use a Cavalier Free Flyte arrow rest with every one of my bows. I shorten the arm a bit so it's stiffer and so it centers the arrow on the side-spring perfectly. When shooting the X10s, I grind down the side-support steel arm to accommodate the extra-small diameter X10 shafts."

Bowstring Serving: "I like the nock pretty snug," says Adams. "I'm serving my center serving about .003-inch thicker than the nock throat. It's firm but it's snug. I serve really tight, using material that doesn't wear much. I use old stuff—a Spectra material with two strands twisted together from Brownell. I take two separate bundles of this and twist them together by hand. So there are actually four strands of Spectra. I can twist it pretty consistently. This serving, despite serious shooting, will last a couple years. I use one single stainless-steel nockset above the arrow nock."

"I like the nock to fit tight," says Nogara. "I reserve all my strings with BCY #62 serving. I use a brass clamp-on nock above the nock, and a little serving string below it. I use the thin stuff. I serve it in, and snug it up against the nock. Without a nock set on the bottom, sometimes your fingers will pull the nock down and you'll shoot high. It's like a fail-safe for me."

Target Panic: "I've had target panic for about seven years and still have it," says Huffman. "I lock in below the target when it flares up. There are things you can do but it isn't right—I keep my bow shooting 1-to-1-½ yards 'hot.' What I mean is I sight it in to shoot a little high. Also, when I practice judging yardage I naturally judge short. A lot of people try to change something in their routine. Once you do that your mind starts thinking about it, and that helps but it's only temporary. The permanent fix is shooting a clicker, in my opinion."

"Once in a while I'll get it," says Nogara. "Instead of continuing I'll go back to the blind bale with 10-to-15 shots and I'll get my mind back to where it was, focusing on the feel of the shot and not where my pin is."

Practice: "Just before hunting season, I'll do different things," says Nogara. "One day is long shots. The next is short shots—the ones guys always miss. I also try to shoot from awkward positions a lot— the same ones I'll face out hunting. I try to mix it up so it doesn't get so boring."

Chuck Adams is a lifelong fingers shooter. He prefers an extra-long bow, with wheels, and low letoff. He's at full draw here using a Reflex Caribou.

As far as my initial grip goes on the bowstring, I make sure the string is bisecting the first crease of my top finger, between the first and second crease in my middle finger, and in the first crease of my third finger. This is the natural position for my fingers when my hand is vertically straight.

"I draw with a deep hook, one above, two below the nock," says Chuck Adams. "Once I come back to full draw and settle in, I actually creep ahead a little bit and ease the string out on the top two fingers. I drop almost all the pressure off the bottom finger—there's only 10 percent or so on this finger, whereas the other two fingers have 45 and 45 percent of the pressure."

"I prefer a two-fingers release, (while) some guys shoot only one," says Mathews Pro Staff member and pro freestyle-limited shooter Rodney Huffman. "Olympic shooters have to use three. To me, two fingers seems more consistent. I drop the top one, and the finger next to my pinkie holds the most pressure. I don't like a deep hook. I grip the string in the first half-joint of my fingers. I believe gripping at the first crease creates finger roll problems."

"I grip at the first crease, then once I hit full draw, the string comes out of the first crease a bit," notes Angelo Nogara, top tournament fingers shooter and expert bowhunter. "When you roll it out a bit, the bowstring 'rips' out of your fingers more. Otherwise, there's a greater chance of plucking it. You also have to shoot lower letoff to get that rip. About halfway down from the tips of my fingers are calluses where the string comes off."

I'd suggest experimenting a great deal with finger pressure to see which type of "hold" yields the most consistency.

Release Technique: Two Schools of Thought

Static Release: Some gifted fingers shooters release the bowstring on command; a visual response that tells their conscious mind when to release. Who am I to say this is the wrong way? However, I believe the method in which you use your entire body to release the arrow, as in using back-tension, offers greater control.

The author continues to enjoy shooting and hunting with a fingers set-up. By utilizing good technique, he made a great shot on this California blacktail buck.

Chuck Adams prefers a command release, and you can't argue with his success. "I shoot the sight like a clicker—when my sight picture is right, I pause a split second and shoot," said Adams. "Average time it takes me from drawing to shooting—three seconds. It's fast but it's deliberate and smooth. There's nothing jerky about it unless I'm doing something wrong."

Dynamic Release: After hours upon hours of deliberate shot training *(with your eyes closed and using back-tension—see Chapter 1)*, you should eventually arrive to a point where your release hand feels like a giant steel hook that is awaiting your body's command to "let the string go." Notice how I said "body" and not "mind."

This technique rests upon the back muscles to trigger the shot, just like the experts teach with a release-aid. This is how it works:

Once you're hooked up, at full draw, and sighting in on target, begin pulling with your draw-side back muscles, slowly moving your entire arm-unit rearward. This induces tension in your back and along the fingers. Keep this tension strong until it's just too much. That's when the shot breaks, taking you by surprise. This style of shooting lessens the chance of target panic or "freezing" of the sight pin as it nears the bull's-eye. You simply allow the sight pin to "roll" around the target, maintaining a strong degree of aiming focus, until the shot goes.

Fact: The moment you think about the release, the shot is ruined.

After the shot, the release hand should move rearward somewhere along your face (caused by the intense pressure). It doesn't matter where it ends up, just be sure it's brushing along your face the whole time. This will keep you from torquing the string horizontally.

1.

2.

3.

Angelo Nogara is a good friend of the author's and an outstanding shot with fingers. Here he demonstrates excellent shooting posture, form and follow-through. He pinches his shoulder blades together as the arrow slips from his relaxed fingers.

"My hand ends up right behind my head," says Huffman. "Fingers should just barely run against the side of your face after the shot. When you don't do that, you pluck, which causes low left and right hits."

"I use the push-pull method of creating back-tension," says Angelo Nogara, a two-time California State Broadhead champion and top NFAA tournament contender. "But I pull a little bit more with my draw-side back muscles. When I get to full draw, I use the kisser to anchor in, and then I'm 'pinching' my shoulder blades together. That's when everything else in my body relaxes, except for my back muscles. If you think about how you're going to release the string, you'll mess up the shot every time. I just keep my shoulder blades pinched and the release goes off. People ask me, when do you know when the release is going off, but I don't know.

"I have a process, a step-method, when I release. First, I watch the arrow flight through my sight, then the bow rocks forward, and then I feel my finger against the side of my face," says Nogara. "If my finger is not in that one spot against the side of my face, I know the shot is bad. If it all comes together I know I've made a great shot."

Practice Time

Most great fingers shooters I know seem to practice religiously, year round. They tell me if they stop shooting for more than a few days, maybe a week, the strength in their fingers and arms tends to weaken to a degree where accuracy suffers somewhat. In a lot of ways, it's like shooting a traditional bow (recurve or longbow) where you must keep muscle memory in peak order, only you happen to be using high-tech gear.

Fingers shooting requires more practice to maintain strength in your fingers and forearms. However, shooting is more fluid-like and there's more of a connection with the bow, so practice rarely feels like a chore.

"During competition I'll shoot every day, for a couple of hours, shooting 100-to-150 arrows," says Huffman. "Yes, I blind bale a lot. I don't recommend shooting long range right from the start. My experience is if you start shooting long range and aren't grouping well you lose confidence. Without self-confidence you have nothing. If I'm holding good, I'll practice a lot at 50 and 60 yards."

"It differs for me," says Nogara. "When I'm preparing for a tournament, I'll shoot every day except Sunday. I might shoot for a couple of hours each day, 200 arrows each time. Sometimes I'll just go out and shoot long distance, but on average, I'll shoot 3 to 4 times a week —minimum—about 200 arrows during each session."

I'll start my shooting with 8-to-10 arrows standing about 6 feet with my eyes closed. I want to get the feel of a smooth release. When I finish practicing that day, I'll do the same thing at the end. I open my shooting the same way I close it, by shooting with my eyes closed."

Fact: More practice is involved with fingers shooting.

The author shot this wilderness elk using a fingers release.

I won't pretty it up. Productive fingers shooting is a difficult, time-consuming process to learn. However, once you have created good shooting form for yourself, and your core shooting muscles are in top shape, most of the hardest work is done. Consistency will follow and you'll enjoy great accuracy using a time-tested shooting method that is a lot of fun and very rewarding. There's just something special about gripping the bow's string using nothing but a leather tab and your own fingers. It emits a very primitive, fluid-like oneness with the bow words cannot describe. That's the splendor behind this form of archery.

TECH TIPS

Related Questions & Answers
By Joe Bell

Best Vanes for Fingers

Question: Are today's tall, compact fletching offerings ideal for fingers shooting? Or are these vanes more suited for release-aids and drop-away rests?

Answer: Any vane will work with fingers given a good arrow rest is used and proper clearance is achieved. However, since this release technique places a lot of natural horizontal torque on the string, you want to stabilize the arrow as quickly as possible once it leaves the bowstring. Fletching (vanes or feathers) with a high degree of surface area and helical that offers the most drag will stabilize the arrow the fastest coming out of the bow. This is critical with fixed-blade broadheads.

Vanes like the Blazer or AAE Max Hunter seem to shoot pretty darn good with mechanical broadheads and the smaller fixed heads. The key with these vanes is to max out the helical for maximum drag. Basically, the smoother your release the less fletching (drag) your arrows require.

Dick Tone, director of Cavalier Archery, told me short vanes are fine for fingers; it all depends on the broadhead used.

However, some experts believe extra-tall, rigid vanes are a mistake with fingers. "We do believe fingers shooters benefit from softer vanes or feathers since some contact with the rest may occur due to the paradox of the arrow," says Bob Mizek, director of engineering for New Archery Products. One way to find out is to simply spray the arrow with foot powder and check for clearance issues.

Bare-Shaft Tuning

Question: A lot of fingers shooters use the bare-shaft tuning method over paper. Which method is best and why?

Answer: There's nothing wrong with bare-shaft tuning. This method works great for identifying the consistency of arrow spine. However, it doesn't truly tell you how the arrow is flying through the air exactly, whereas paper will. With a broadhead, you want absolutely straight arrow flight to maximize arrow penetration, forgiveness and accuracy. I recommend following the tuning procedure discussed in chapter 6, which involves the use of paper and shooting the arrow at various distances to identify a perfect tear using a broadhead-tipped arrow.

Drop-Away Rests

A good arrow rest is vital for top fingers accuracy. This Cavalier Free-Flyte and Cavalier Master-Lok Plunger is one of the best set-ups available.

Another favorite arrow rest used by the author is the New Archery Flipper II, used in conjunction with a Cavalier Master-Lok Plunger. This stick-on rest can accommodate modern-style bow risers by using a thin plate of aluminum or plastic, glued in place using contact cement. It's very simple, quiet and deadly accurate.

Question: I was thinking about trying a drop-away style arrow rest that offers side support. What are your thoughts on using this kind of rest with fingers?

continued on next page...

Answer: According to many arrow rest engineers, drop-away rests aren't the best with fingers. "We've not had good luck with fingers and drop-away rests, and we have tested the competition," says Bob Mizek, director of engineering for New Archery Products. "We believe that unless the archer is able to release the arrow very cleanly with little paradox, there just is not sufficient guidance (time-wise) to get good consistency."

The other downside to these rests is that they don't offer fine-tuning of the side support arm, where you can stiffen or weaken it. That's the upside to the flipper/plunger style rest; it's fully adjustable.

Also, I've spent a lot of hours watching Easton's slow-motion video of arrows coming out of various bows, particularly those released using a fingers release. I'd say in most cases, fingers released arrows stay in contact with the arrow rest the first 8 inches or so of the arrow launch, then arrow paradox takes over. However, during the last phase of the bending of the arrow, it sometimes makes contact with the arrow rest once again. For this reason, a rest without long-term side cushioning can prove less accurate for a fingers-released arrow.

Arrow Spine

Question: Do you think all-aluminum arrows are the No. 1 choice for fingers since these shafts have the best spine consistency?

Answer: Spine consistency is crucial for fingers shooters, since the arrow bends so much coming out of the bow. All-aluminum is an excellent choice, however, today's aluminum/carbon arrows are just as good. Easton ACC arrows are among the most consistent I've ever tested, on par with Easton XX78 aluminum arrows.

Also, many of today's all-carbon offerings seem to produce superb accuracy with fingers, which is testimony of their spine consistency. I've achieved great accuracy with fixed-blade broadheads using Easton Axis, Carbon Tech Whitetail XP, and Carbon Express Maxima Hunter shafts. I do admit seeing a few more "flyers" among all-carbon shafts, but again, it all depends on the brand. I suggest numbering your arrows and noting impact patterns. Any irregular patterns will show you which shafts to cull out—these are likely off in spine from the others.

Using a Clicker

Question: I've thought of using a clicker to control my target panic. Do you recommend one for hunting?

Answer: Personally, I don't think clickers cure target panic—they can take the edge off when shooting at targets, but in hunting they become a bit more complicated.

I believe clickers work best in those situations where the archer is tired of dealing with the ruts of his old shooting style. The clicker, in this case, can bring in a whole new dimension. But the shooter must realize that this new shooting accessory and style will take lots and lots of time to master. Most archers are looking for a fast fix—but there really aren't any shortcuts in archery.

Bell shot this central-barren ground caribou in the Northwest Territories, Canada, while using a clicker on his bow.

A "Band-Aid" will only provide temporary relief.

At first, a clicker may seem to eliminate freezing completely, but it won't be permanent. Soon you'll be accustomed to the new shooting style and once this normalcy sets in, it's easy for you to fall into the same shooting habits as before. Why? Because you haven't changed your mental approach on how you shoot. The key, I believe, is to begin fresh and create an entirely new mindset to go along with your new shooting style. Become more disciplined in how you practice—practice in an orderly fashion, focusing on exact, consistent shooting form, and shooting well and building confidence. That's how you control target panic. In other words, you should keep shooting the clicker until the process becomes totally ingrained (this could take a long time—6 months, a year, or more).

Years ago I hunted with a clicker...I successfully "clicked off" on animals a small percentage of the time, mainly on longer shots where the emotional intensity was less. The thing that bothered me most about a clicker was that during those instances when I was holding solidly on target but didn't click off, the arrow would shoot pretty far off target, instead of coming close, like it would with a non-clicker set-up (despite slight creeping). I guess this is because of the draw and cam dynamics on modern eccentrics from that extra ¼-inch of draw it takes to activate the clicker (which is where the bow was sighted-in).

Overall, clickers are difficult to use in hunting situations and even harder yet with modern bows, which have aggressive draw cycles and narrow valleys. Because of this, they tend to create more problems than they solve out hunting. In target shooting, I think they have their place, though most "hunter" fingers classes won't allow them.

The audible "click" of a clicker is helpful in creating a surprise shot. However, you can create another type of non-audible cue that will prove nearly as helpful. For example, tell yourself you cannot shoot unless you tighten up your back, pinch your shoulder blades together, move your elbow, or feel some movement in your index finger or the back of your hand after a solid anchor is achieved (all of these indicate the use of back-tension). I have found all of these helpful in creating a delayed, surprise-style release that is easy to use in a hunting situation. Even the idea of staying on target for at least 2-to-3 seconds before allowing yourself to shoot can be a very helpful, relaxing shooting cue.

Nock Locator and Height

Question: My fingers bow seems to shoot well with a nock height of about one-half inch. Is this too high? Also, do you use a standard metal clamp-on or a tie-in nockset?

Answer: I've had some bows tune with a nock height just over one-half inches, but that was with the first-generation one-cam bows. Most modern bows will tune well about 3/8-inch above center, give or take 1/16-inch or so, plus or minus. It just depends on the cam system and bow geometry.

I still use a standard clamp-on nockset, but I'm experimenting with tie-in nocks. Many of the best fingers shooters I know use tie-in nocksets, one above and below the nock. I've tried this arrangement, but I can't seem to snap the arrow on without looking, the way that I can with a single metal clamp-on nockset. I do believe using two nocksets has the potential to increase accuracy, however. Right now I'm using a clamp-on nockset above the arrow nock and a tie-in nockset below.

Where to Anchor

Question: Most modern fingers shooters I know anchor low, with the string at the tip of their nose. I still anchor at the corner of my mouth using my index finger. Should I switch?

Answer: It doesn't matter where you anchor as long as it's consistent and accurate. One summer I experimented with a lower anchor to increase my sight-pin window. However, after a couple months, I switched back to the old tried-and-true—index finger in the corner of my mouth. My groups were better this way. The key I found was keeping the web area made up by my index finger and thumb solidly braced against my jaw. With a lower anchor, my thumb (or lower portion of the web) was floating, which I believe affected my consistency.

Arrow/Tip Weight and FOC

Question: What's the best arrow set-up and FOC combination for fingers shooting?

Answer: Fingers shooting and heavier arrows go hand in hand—the heavier the arrow, the smoother the takeoff, and the more forgiving the set-up. Stick with arrows that weigh 8.5 grains per inch or more for best all-around performance.

Also, a heavier FOC weight is advisable. More FOC gives the arrow a quicker recovery time. When you release an arrow with fingers, a side-to-side movement occurs known as archer's paradox. For a right-hand shooter, the nock-end of the arrow actually kicks to the left, and then swings to the right, then back to the left again as it passes the arrow rest and riser. It continues in this fishtail pattern the first few yards or so, until the spine and fletching of the arrow correct the movement. With a heavier FOC, the arrow becomes more stable in flight during this critical moment, directing your arrow down a consistent path. Arrows with higher FOC are more stable in the wind for the same reason—the arrows correct sooner once the wind induces airflow from the side, wagging the arrow.

Chapter 9
Equipment Insights

Those Small Things That Can Really Add Up

"Great things are not done by impulse, but by a series of small things brought together."
—Vincent Van Gogh

Shooting confidence is the most important component in becoming a successful bow-hunter. According to the author, it's the "smaller" things we learn through intense shooting, tuning, sampling various equipment, and through mental training exercises that will give us that extra edge.

After years of shooting, I've come to realize it's the small things that make all the difference in shooting success and/or confidence. It is only through years of experience, learning by trial and error that you come across certain details that accelerate you as a shooter. But there is another way to enhance this learning curve, and that is by paying attention to what the experts do. This approach is not cheating; it's just being smart.

The following people are some of the best release shooters I've come across. They all have strong backgrounds in tournament archery, but they are also extremely successful bowhunters, so you know what they have to say is applicable to the deer woods, which is what this book is all about—giving you that technical edge as a bowhunter.

Here are some of these experts' key traits and tips regarding shooting techniques and gear. I would strongly consider their advice or equipment preferences—years of thought and trial and error have gone into these choices. Also realize that these same folks socialize with other "elite" shooters on a regular basis and compare notes on what does and does not work.

Randy Ulmer

Ulmer needs no introduction; he's one of the most renowned bowhunters in the industry. He holds many past record titles as a pro-level 3-D, indoor/outdoor shooter, and continues to make huge headlines throughout the print bowhunting media as one of the most successful hunters in the West; his expertise and bowhunting ability on trophy mule deer and elk has become legendary.

Randy Ulmer's success in the field is incredible. He's pictured with another huge Nevada mule deer.

Shooting Tips: "When coming to full draw, I like to bring the string and peep to my face—not the other way around," says Ulmer. "Some bowhunters seem to 'crawl' into the bow with their face to anchor."

When Randy hits full draw, his correct sight pin is nearly on the spot. When hunting, he looks intently at the target during the draw and sight acquisition phase.

"When I draw back on a buck, my entire focus is on determining exactly where I want to aim and making sure I aim using the right pin," he says. "I try to eliminate every possible little tolerance there is in the shot. If the deer is 38 yards away, I don't want to aim with my 40-yard pin in the middle…I want that pin precisely where it needs to be for a 38-yard hit. The more precise I am about every aspect of the shot, the less chance there is for something to go wrong."

Practice Routine: "When I begin shooting in the spring, I spend the first few days shooting with my eyes closed to focus on the feeling of the perfect shot," says Ulmer. "It usually only takes a few days to feel like I'm making a relaxed shot using good form. If I try to get the same feeling while shooting at a target, it may take weeks. Also, I tend to avoid any bad habits from surfacing if I start with my eyes closed.

"I practice a great deal in the summer. However, during hunting season I'm usually so busy with the actual hunt or catching up with work when I get home that I don't practice much. But, when I'm on a hunt I insist on shooting at least one arrow a day to make sure my bow is sighted and to boost my confidence if I do get a shot at game."

Long-Range Shooting/Sight Movement: "At long range, everyone's sight will drift in and out of the target. Everyone has a certain amount of movement. However, there's a fine line between 'I'm in the bull's-eye and so I'm going to pull a little harder with my back muscles and increase trigger tension,' to, 'Okay, I'm now back in the bull's-eye and so I'm going to HAMMER IT!' When I'm drifting in and out of the target, I do increase tension on the trigger when the sight picture is good."

Hunting Arrows: "I like to shoot a medium-weight arrow. I can shoot one at about 280 fps with my fairly long draw length. By today's standards, I would consider 400 grains fairly heavy. I use a 26-inch arrow. I like shorter arrows because they drift less in the wind. I use an overdraw. Shorter arrows are also stiffer. Stiffer arrows seem to tune better and shoot with greater forgiveness, particularly with broadheads."

Bow Tuning: "I've found the bows that shoot a perfect bullet hole through paper are the most forgiving. That's what I strive for. If it doesn't tune, it won't be my number one or two bow. This applies to my hunting and target bows."

"When tuning a drop-away rest, I want it to stay up as long as possible but it must not hit the fletching. I spray my arrows to determine where it needs to drop for the fletching to clear."

String Loops: "String-loop length depends on the type of release and anchor you use. If your release hooks on your loop perpendicularly, you can use a shorter and a stiffer loop. If you twist your release at all, however, you need a flexible material."

"With my Carter Quickie hunting release, I use a fairly stiff material and it's not that long. But with my back-tension release, I use a longer, more flexible loop material."

"I tie in a nockset below the nock using BCY's braided nylon."

When Shooting in the Wind: "The biggest variable in accuracy is not how well you can shoot a bow. It's in your ability to shoot an arrow that bucks the wind and your ability to judge the wind."

Randy shoots a 26-inch Easton Full Metal Jacket arrow, 100-grain Rage broadhead, and low-profile 2-inch AAE Plastifletch Max vanes, which are mounted at maximum helical to get the arrow spinning as quickly as possible. He's done extensive testing under windy conditions and he believes this is the ultimate arrow combination for such conditions. However, he doesn't recommend this set-up to all shooters since the smaller vanes don't provide as much control/accuracy when "rough" releases occur. "I think some bowhunters are better off with larger vanes, such as 4-inch standard vanes or 2-inch Max Hunter vanes. These are more forgiving."

Releases: Ulmer uses a backtension release, a Carter model, for all his target shooting and practice shooting up until a few weeks before hunting season. Then he switches to a Carter Quickie 2. The trigger tension is set very light on this release.

Hunting Bow Preferences: "I use 65-percent letoff for target shooting and hunting. I feel the advantages of a using a low letoff bow are more than offset by their disadvantages. Low letoff is simply more forgiving. Forgiveness is my main criteria for hunting. I take very few shots from a normal in-your-backyard stand-up position. Most shots are off-balance, especially when you're sneaking around and trying to hide. To yield greater forgiveness you have to use a longer axle-length bow. I'm shooting a Hoyt Vectrix XL at 70 pounds, 36 inches axle to axle. It has a 7 ½-inch brace height."

Derek Phillips

As a past pro-level 3-D and outdoor/indoor tournament archer, Phillips is a superb shot. However, he's also a serious bowhunter who regularly takes incredible mule deer and whitetail bucks, as well as elk and antelope. Also, as the pro-staff manager for Mathews

Derek Phillips runs Mathews' Pro Staff Division. Each year he puts his shooting expertise to good use, whether on the range or in the field.

Archery, Phillips coordinates one of the winningest groups of pro shooters in the world. Consequently, he knows a lot about the sport and just what it takes to succeed.

Releases: "I use a Carter Target 3 for competition, which has a thumb release/hammer. I use this release very similar to how you would shoot a back-tension release. I generally pull against the wall of the draw and pull through the shot, allowing pressure to be applied on the hammer by my thumb in a pulling-pressure motion versus the rotating motion of a hinged back-tension release. Basically, I try to hold the front arm steady, while pulling through."

"For hunting, I use the same release for the most part; except if I expect to have to make snap shots, then I like a trigger release. My favorites are the Carter Two-Shot or the Scott Little Goose. I have tremendous amounts of confidence in these two releases as they have very clean triggering mechanisms. The Tru-Ball Short and Sweet also falls in this category. For my sight-in and practice for hunting I shoot the Target 3 for the most part, only switching to the trigger release if I expect to use it. The change over for me is very easy, probably from years of practice with the trigger. Thus, after a few shots I'm usually ready to go."

Anchor: "I rest my release hand lightly against my face, with the back of my hand turned-toward my face with the Carter Target 3 release. When I shoot a trigger release, the pressure is a little heavier and with the area between my thumb and first finger resting against my face. With the Target 3, the back of my hand covers my ear area and with the trigger release, the anchor is lower, down below my ear almost."

Aiming: "I attempt to draw my bow with the pin pointed right at where I intend to hit. This does several things for me. First, it reduces the amount of movement I have when drawing and aiming the bow in a hunting situation. Secondly, I've found that target panic can sometimes creep into play when people use the above or below methods of approach with the pin.

"When shooting targets, once I start aiming I don't think about anything else. In fact, if I do have another thought creep into my mind during that process, I stop the shot and let down. During hunting, I tend to watch the animal's body language during the aiming process to detect any type of perceived danger or moment that may occur prior to the shot."

"My focus is primarily on the sight pin, with a small amount of concentration on the aiming location. I center the sight housing with my peep and then reference my pin after that. This method, in my opinion, is more consistent, due to the reference area that is used. Whereas if you just use your pin in the middle of your peep, then my question is are you sure it is in the middle every time?"

Shot time: "For competition, usually the shot window is about 4-to-6 seconds. In a hunting scenario, it can be much less depending on the circumstances. However, under ideal situations, I'd prefer that it be somewhere in the 3-to-5 second range."

String Loops: "Most of the time I prefer a D-loop, however, depending on the tune of a bow, I have used a loop under arrangement, where the nock sits above both loop knots, and then a regular tie-in nocking point (preferably waxed string that I melt into place) is above the arrow's nock. Using a loop takes away any torque that I might put into the release during a pressure situation, adding to a more consistent shot."

Shot Warm-Up: "When I was competing, my warm up was about 45-to-60 minutes on a blank bale at about three yards. I focused on nothing more that the anchor point, release and follow-through of the shot. More than anything it was to develop in the subconscious what a good shot was every time so it would be second nature during a tournament or at the moment of truth when hunting."

"After that, I usually shot at 40, 50 and 60 yards. I would finish my practice at 20 yards to build confidence before I stopped for the day. Next, I spent twice the amount of time judging yardage, which I attribute most of my success in the 3-D professional ranks to that effort.

"For hunting, most of my shooting practice was much shorter. Usually, I shot the hunting set up at 20 and 30 yards. I did this, because that was where most of my hunting shots occurred.

I wore hunting apparel when possible, with face nets and other hunting essentials. I've always been a proponent of practicing under the same conditions you are likely to face out hunting."

Bow Set-Up: "I use either a Mathews Apex 7 bow, 65 percent letoff or Mathews Drenalin, 80-percent letoff, 68 pounds. I usually use a three-arrow quiver, sometimes five depending on the hunt, which I keep on the bow with arrows in it, even for practice. (For practice, I do remove the first arrow from the quiver and shoot like that for the entire practice session).

"My draw length is just under 29 inches. Release type and style can affect this slightly. For competition now I usually draw around 61 or 62 pounds. My draw length for hunting remains the same or slightly shorter if anything. I prefer to hunt with about 67 or 68 pounds of draw weight."

Common Form Flaws: "The most common flaw I see is an inconsistent anchor, shooting too much bow weight and the draw length being too long. All are very common, with some people doing all of them."

Tuning: "Most of the time I bare-shaft tune, versus using paper. I usually do this out to about 5 yards, where by then the fletching should have established control of the shaft providing consistent flight as long as the onset of the flight of the bare shaft is good."

"Tiller tune of a one cam is simple, back the limbs out equally with the limb bolts. Most archers prefer to shoot the bow with the limbs all the way in at max poundage, thus eliminating this issue. However, with low or high tears that I don't feel are associated with an arrow or rest issue, I will turn one limb out or in a half of a turn to see if it changes that tear indication. In my case in bare-shaft tuning, I'm looking for an indication from the rear of the shaft after impact in a target. A perfect tune means it is planted straight into the target, not canted to the left or right."

BY JOE BELL

Mike Slinkard

Mike Slinkard is president of Winner's Choice Bowstrings. Not only is he a top contender on the pro-level tournament circuit, but he's also an amazing bowhunter. He's well known for his expertise on bow set-up.

A passionate shooter and bowhunter, Slinkard continues to compete as a pro shooter in a variety of circuits, including IBO 3-D, NFAA indoor and outdoor, and ESPN's Great Outdoor Games. He's also the owner and president of Winner's Choice Bowstrings. I consider him one of the most knowledgeable guys on shooting technique and bow set-up.

Practicing/Warm-Up: "For me, when preparing for hunting, I usually start out immediately with mental visualization, which is basically envisioning an actual life-like 'hunting shot.' I cannot normally warm up in the field, so I do not see an advantage to practicing that way either. As for shot distance I try to vary that greatly from 20-to-80 yards and especially practicing on the 'off yardages' (those that I must gap between 2 pins). After 100 shots or so of this I do like to go to 90 or 100 yards and shoot some purely form shots just to make sure that my form and equipment is working properly.

"During season, it is usually much more difficult to follow the same routine. I do try to shoot at least a couple of times a week during the season just to check equipment and such. I still do the mental practice, however, just picturing the quarry presenting a shot, and me making it. Some may call it daydreaming, but I believe it really helps keep me ready for the moment of truth.

"As for long range, I usually do shoot long distance (60-to-80 yards) right from the start, and do shoot a lot (probably 70 percent) from those distances. For me, if I am confident at 80 yards, it makes a 40-yard shot seem like a piece of cake. Please realize that I always strive to get as close as possible in the field, but being confident at long range makes the closer shots easy."

Broadheads: "In my experience with proper equipment set-up and tuning, most of the current high-end fixed-blade heads can be as accurate as field points or mechanicals, and will hit the same spot as field points. Since it is illegal here in Oregon to use mechanicals, I have been forced to learn what it takes to make the fixed-blade head shoot as accurately as possible.

"I have had good success with arrow speeds up to 310 fps with my fixed-blade heads. The most important thing is that the head must be absolutely straight with the shaft. I attain this with a tool that I made from an arrow straightener, which I use to align heads to 1/1000th of an inch. It is amazing the difference this can make, especially in broadhead group size. I have found that heads that look aligned using the old spin test (putting the point against a fixed dot and spinning it to look for wobble) can be 20/1000ths or more off. This makes a big difference in long-range accuracy.

"Also, bow tuning and arrow spine are much more important with fixed heads, but I have always been able to attain the same point of impact and the same group size from my fixed heads now for many years. I simply do not stop tuning until I achieve this goal. My current hunting arrow is the Gold tip 22 series that is really over recommended spine, but I have found that with fixed heads too stiff is much better than too weak.

"As for tuning, most of the time very minor rest adjustments will do the trick. I am now using Spot Hogg's new Whammy rest, and this rest is by far the best in achieving my accuracy goals with broadheads.

"I think that mechanical heads have come a long way in the past few years; however, considering the fact that I can get the same accuracy from my fixed heads, I do not see any reason to gamble with a mechanical, which may not work properly or will achieve less than full pass-through penetration."

Arrows: "I shoot pretty light arrows for all my game, and really feel like the arrow weight issue is overblown in most cases. With heads that are *truly* sharp I have had absolutely no penetration problems with lighter arrows. Currently my arrows are not really pushing the envelope weight wise as they once were at 390 grains (70 pounds at 28 inches), but for many years I had great success with 350-grain arrows on all animals up to moose. Probably 90 percent of the animals I shoot are pass-throughs unless the arrow hits heavy bone like the shoulder socket in which case no arrow will penetrate.

"Broadhead sharpness is responsible in a lot of ways for the penetration of the arrow. I have not found a single head that I consider sharp enough to hunt with right out of the package. I insist on ultimate sharpness that must be obtained by working the blades myself. I think that this is probably the single biggest reason I almost always get complete penetration."

Tuning: "I start with paper, and with a one-cam bow want about ½-inch high left tear. With hybrids and two-cam bows I like a bullet hole. I cannot really explain why this is on the single-cam bows, but for me at least it will almost always yield better groups."

"Paper is only the start. The real test, however, is long-range group tuning with broadheads. Usually I do this at 60 or 70 yards and make final small adjustments. I also shoot three broadheads and two field points when I am doing this so I can be sure they hit together. I spend a lot of time at this stage as I consider this the most important part of equipment preparation.

"Once I get it all dialed in then I 'blueprint' the bow by recording all pertinent specs and mark the cam position so I can return the bow to the exact same position should any unforeseen problem occur. This saved me a lot of time just this year when my bowstring accidentally rubbed against a bracket on my ATV and cut it in two. I was able to replace the string, and return the bow to pinpoint accuracy in less than an hour, and was back in the field."

Aiming/Sight Movement: "I think everyone's sight has some movement, but I do everything I can to get it as still as possible. If you have your release happening in the subconscious like it should be the movement should really have no effect on the shot as the subconscious will trigger the shot when the pin is on the target. Just look at the spot and trust your subconscious to do what you trained it to."

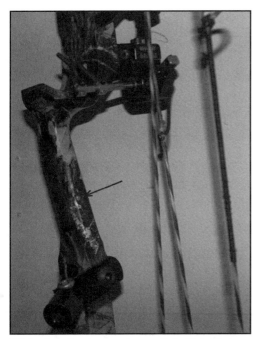

Slinkard prefers to mount a small stud into his bow grips. This way he knows how to position his hand exactly the same way on each and every shot.

Shooting in the Wind: "This one is really tough, and really comes from experience. My outdoor range is in a very windy area so, unfortunately, I get the opportunity to practice in the wind a lot more than I would prefer. I just get a feel for the wind velocity and hold off accordingly. Wind is one thing that will greatly limit the distance I am willing to shoot in the field as it can have a huge effect not only from an arrow-drift standpoint, but more so from the tension it imparts on your bow arm during the shot, effectively deteriorating shooting form."

Straight-on Shots: "The head-on shot at big game is really not an option for me at anything over 15 yards, if then. There is simply too much that can go wrong, and too little margin for error. Done perfectly this is a devastating shot, but veer only slightly left or right and impact will turn the arrow outside the rib cage and result in a wounding loss.

The way I look at it, unless the animal actually runs over you, it has to turn to give you a better angle and a much higher percentage shot."

Releases: "I use a Carter Quickie for all my hunting. For me a back-tension release is only for target shooting, and is simply not adaptable enough for me to hunt with. I need to make a shot happen when it presents itself, and with back-tension that is much harder to achieve."

"I shoot my hunting release the same way I do a target rifle as far as trigger pull goes. I have very light trigger tension, and it takes very little pressure to activate the shot. With my method, I set my back-tension when I reach full draw—that gives me the best hold—then slowly add pressure to the trigger. As I have said many times, the actual adding of the pressure is controlled by the subconscious mind and is not something I actually think about when shooting. For me, a light trigger best allows my subconscious to trigger the shot at the correct time. My finger is lightly in contact with the trigger once I am ready to shoot.

"I shoot my Spot-Hogg Saturday Night Special release for all my target shooting except Buckmasters and our Motion Target pop-ups where I use my hunting release. I shoot it with the exact same mental steps as my hunting release except that the trigger is activated with the thumb instead of the forefinger. I use a wrist strap on this release that holds all the weight of the bow at full draw and provides a solid hold on target. This release can be set lighter than any other I have found and provides extreme control for my subconscious. Beginning about late June, I switch to my hunting release for the most of my shooting. This release is easier to load in hunting situations and is also extremely accurate."

Bows: "For me, I used to always look for at least a 38-inch bow, but nowadays with the parallel limbs the axle lengths I am using are shorter. Currently, I am shooting a Ross Cardiac at 34 inches and shooting it exceptionally well. I do like to keep the brace height at no less than 6 ½, and 7 inches is better. I like 80 percent letoff for hunting, as I think it is just a little easier when you have to hold a long time waiting for the shot to develop, and also for me I hold the lighter weight a little more stable."

"Always the biggest concern is accuracy and forgiveness in my hunting bows. Speed is great too, but not as important as accuracy. It try to get a little of both but always if it comes down to a choice I will go toward accuracy every time."

Bow Grips: "The thinner the better on the grip. The first thing that comes off my bows is the grip, even side-plates on the two-piece grip designs. Thin narrow grips are simply harder to induce torque to the bow. I think of it like the handle on a screwdriver. If you want to install a big screw and need a lot of torque, you can get this easier by using a big handled screwdriver. The same principal is true in a bow grip. The smaller the grip the less surface you have to add torque. I do not put anything on my grip where my hand actually contacts the bow. I may add some fleece stick on material to the front of the grip just to make it a little more comfortable when carrying it, but nothing on the contact area of the grip.

"Now I do one thing to my grips that I feel makes a big difference in accuracy. I actually install a small 'stud' in my grips in a location that coincides with the area where I want the pressure to be concentrated in my hand. This stud does not cause any pain in the hand; it just serves as an unmistakable location on the grip for my hand. I have found that this greatly increases my accuracy and consistency, especially in hunting situations where you may be in an odd position, cold, or otherwise distracted."

Bow Quiver Accuracy: "I always use a bow-mounted quiver for hunting. The main reason is arrow accessibility, as I have never liked the idea of a hip or back quiver from the standpoint of ease of use. A bow quiver does have one major downside in my mind, and that is in the wind it does make the bow rock around.

"As far as balance on some of my bows I use a v-bar with a single-side mounted weight to help compensate for the quiver. I always practice with four arrows in my quiver (I use a 5-arrow quiver), since this is the situation that the bow is in 99 percent of the time in a hunting situation. I really do not see a lot of difference with three arrows in the quiver either, maybe a little with fewer arrows in the quiver. My choice on this is just that I am not really willing to sacrifice the ease of use of the bow quiver for the little bit of accuracy gain that it may or may not yield."

Darin Cooper

Darin Cooper is a very talented engineer, target shooter and bowhunter. He spends a tremendous amount of time analyzing the most accurate gear and shooting technique.

Whether the game is pro-level indoor/outdoor target archery, 3-D, ESPN's Great Outdoor Games speed-shooting, or stalking big-game in the West, Cooper proves himself as one of the most passionate players in the world. Because of this, he's quite accomplished in every one of these categories. He's also the Senior Product Design Engineer at Hoyt USA, who was instrumental in designing Hoyt's revolutionary Cam & ½ bow eccentric system. A meticulous engineer, he takes bow set-up, shooting and equipment very seriously.

Cooper likes to pull into the bow's wall once he hits full draw, then he anchors, centers the pin in the peep, and begins the aiming process. He prefers to focus on the aiming spot, not the pin.

Shooting: "Once I reach full draw, I pull into the wall about 3-to-4 pounds, anchor, center the pin in the peep, level the bow, and then allow the pin to fall onto the spot. I always draw slightly above the target. I then wrap my thumb around the trigger and apply about 90 percent of the pressure required to execute the shot. At this point I focus intently on the exact place I want the arrow to hit while pulling through the shot using back-tension, monitoring the position of the pin with my subconscious. If the pin is not where it needs to be, I'll let the shot down.

"Under certain hunting conditions, I'll double pump the shot. If I'm forced to stay at full draw, I'll exhale and take another breath or multiple breaths so my system can recover until the shot develops. When it's time, I quickly inhale and pull through the shot."

Practice Routine: "During hunting season, I practice almost exclusively with broadheads at 60-to-90 yards. I shoot a lot of arrows to ensure my equipment is performing up to my expectations. Most importantly, I want to make sure that the strings and cables are well shot in, my sight is perfectly sighted in, and my sight marks and windage are consistent day to day. I'll shoot 60-to-100 shots daily for a couple weeks prior to a hunt, 2-to-3 days/week until the week prior. I probably shoot daily leading up to the hunt. I absolutely despise missing animals! During the hunt I try to shoot at least a dozen shots per day to ensure my bow is still dialed in because it sees a ton of wear and abuse.

"I don't do much warm-up. It's probably a good idea, but mine is limited to quickly stretching my drawing muscles and back muscles and flexing my joints just to ensure they're lubricated and ready to handle the load before the first arrow."

Broadheads: "I doubt there's any real ceiling to velocity when it comes to fixed blades, but I think all the right elements must be in place for a fixed-blade tipped arrow to perform well. I've accurately shot fixed-blade heads at 303 fps out to 100 yards. Without a doubt, tuning, arrow straightness, spine around the shaft (SAS), form, and broadhead alignment become more critical above 280 fps. My Wac'-Em tipped, 456-grain Easton Full Metal Jacket arrows were coming out of my 2008 Hoyt at 290 fps. It's a tack driver out to 110 yards! The Wac'-Em shoots incredibly well and out-groups almost every fixed-blade head I've shot. It's got a relatively mild blade angle and a cut-on-impact tip that contribute to maximum penetration. I think it's the best fixed-blade head on the market."

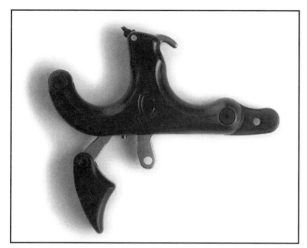

Most pro shooters use a T-handle release for the majority of their shooting. Such releases tend to have better triggers. Cooper uses an older model of the Carter Ember, which he uses for all shooting applications, including hunting.

Arrow FOC Weight: "Heavier shafts drift less in the wind, and more FOC seems to improve my groups. I have worked hard to find ways to get 150 grains in the front of my broadhead tipped arrows. I've recently added a second HIT insert into my Easton Axis FMJs to get me to 157 grains of point weight (16-grain insert x 2 + 125 grain broadhead = 157). Previously I would tap the insert through on my A/C/C 3-49s and add a 20-grain 8-32 setscrew to get approximately 150 grains of point weight. I will run a test in the coming months to show the difference in my groups with 157 up front versus 116. I can't guarantee the outcome as it relates to this, but every time I've tried it in the past I've tightened my fixed-blade groups dramatically with the heavier set-up."

Back-tension: "Use the draw side only… don't push out with the bow arm. It will add movement and a lot of unnecessary tension in the bow shoulder. The bow arm should remain relaxed and just accept the load as if you were leaning against the wall with your hand."

Tuning: "I spend a fair amount of time tuning my bows, but I know all the tricks of set-up so it rarely takes long. I'm looking for a bullet hole through paper from all distances with a bare shaft before I even shoot a fletched arrow. I don't freak out if the bow, rest, or arrow won't allow the arrow to shoot perfectly. I'll shoot the bow and see if it groups if I can't get a perfect tear. I'll analyze the shape of the groups I'm shooting and move either the nocking point height for a vertical group or the center shot for a horizontal group until it tightens up. In some cases I'll shoot a conventional prong rest, because they give you a little more capability for tuning out high/low tears.

"I also like to shoot a bare shaft at a target now and then to see if it will shoot with the fletched shafts. On my best shooting set-ups I can shoot bare shafts in the 10-ring at 70 meters. Everything has to be perfect for this to happen."

Arrow Nock Fit: "I prefer a tight nock fit over a loose-fitting nock. I also like to tie nock sets inside the D-Loop on my bows to minimize pinch. I like my serving to be about .110-inch for a large groove .098-inch nock throat. When hanging the arrow from the string, a light tap should disengage the nock. I don't like any wobble or up and down slop between my tied nocks."

Long-Range Shooting: "My pin will stay in or near the spot the majority of the time. It may drift toward the edges and a little way off where I'm aiming, but if I don't feel like I have an excellent chance of hitting what I'm aiming at, I'm not going to shoot the shot. Once I aim, I like to continue the process with the intent of shooting the shot unless the pin goes well away from the center (especially low) at which point I'll probably let down. I've let down on animals as many as four times because I couldn't get steady on a tough shot.

"I find that the longer you hold the more likely you are to make a poor shot. This is more obvious when shooting at long-range with broadheads. When I'm facing a tough shot I like to be aggressive by pre-loading hard into the wall and pulling hard through the release. One of my biggest keys is trying to mentally burn a hole in the target. The smaller the detail I can pick out and focus on, the tighter my groups will be. Four or five seconds of aiming before the release fires is what I hope for. This also means that once I get the pin to the spot, the shot happens quickly and doesn't allow for the shot to deteriorate. Target archers get in trouble on tough shots when they try to baby the arrow into the spot—just step up and shoot it like you own it.

"Another reason that I don't like to overhold a shot is that you will actually lose velocity out of your bow as you hold the shot because the buss cable will temporarily elongate under the tension reducing the draw weight. Try it in front of a chronograph. The cable will quickly recover its length once the shot is fired, but your arrow will most likely hit a little low if you over-hold."

Releases: "I shoot a handheld Carter Ember year round (actually it's a Gitterdun that they only made 30 of, which is very similar to the Ember). I do not like switching up releases often. I shoot this for target so it's easiest for me to shoot what I've used for 15,000 arrows already during my target practice. I think most bowhunters should stick with one release regardless of whether they shoot a hinge-style back-tension release or a caliper. Use the same for target, practice, and hunting. I will occasionally train with the Carter Evolution Mini to ensure that I'm pulling through the shot properly."

"My releases are set up relatively heavy. I don't like a hair trigger. Many people get confused between trigger travel and trigger pull. My pull is heavy but there is virtually no travel. I usually re-spring all my releases to get about 2-½ pounds of trigger pull. Sometimes I actually use shims and mix and match parts to get an absolutely crisp consistent trigger. Your release is one of the most important pieces of equipment—probably the most difficult to change out and stay shooting well. I always have at least one, and usually two back-up releases that are virtually identical. I use a digital scale to measure and match trigger pull."

Section 3

Specialized Advice

Chapter 10
No Shot Too Challenging

Make Impossible Shots Happen

*"The real price of everything, what everything really costs to the man who wants to
acquire it, is the toil and trouble of acquiring it."*
—*Adam Smith*

With the right knowledge and shot practice, you can make extreme-angled shots
in the field.

Shooting ability is one thing, but knowledge of your arrow's trajectory in a variety of situations is just as important for making successful shots in the field. Like most bowhunters, I've executed some pretty good shots over the years while hunting big game, however, many of these arrows missed the mark by a long shot. That was because I was clueless about arrow trajectory, and lacked the knowledge to compensate for extreme shooting angles.

Here are the ins and outs of extreme bow shooting and how you can eliminate much of the difficulty.

Steep Shots: Gravity's Effect

When practicing in your backyard, your line of sight is level, so your sight pins are set according to the horizontal effects of gravity. However, the more angled the arrow's flight path is, as in shooting up or downhill, the less affect gravity has on the arrow, if very much at all. This means you must subtract, even on uphill shots, from the actual viewing distance. This adds a whole new dimension—and a confusing one at that—to the world of bow shooting, and it is the culprit of many unfortunate misses each season.

Yet, with a bit of knowhow, practice and reference, you can make these shots with amazing precision. It's really simpler than you think.

In the past, I would usually "feel" my way through these shots. Basically, I'd take a 3-D target into some canyon country and begin a repertoire of shooting drills, at extreme uphill and downhill. From this practice, I'd gain some idea of how to aim for these shots. However, as shot distances went beyond 35 yards or so and as angles got steeper, shooting accuracy quickly took a turn for the worse. Your eyes can fool you. Thus, this method is not the most reliable. It may work well for fast shots at relatively close range, or when shooting from a tree-stand, but under many other conditions you will probably find that it misses the mark.

Fact: Arrows will strike high, whether you shoot up or downhill.

Fortunately, there is a more precise way of handling extreme shots: you can buy one of today's laser rangefinders with a built-in angle compensator feature, or you can calculate the angle and shooting distance yourself by using a standard laser rangefinder, pocket inclinometer (angle meter) and "cut" chart reference tool.

I recommend becoming well versed in the latter technique (using a pocket inclinometer) and the percentage in which you'll have to subtract from the line-of-sight distance. Otherwise, you're becoming totally reliant on an electronic, battery-operated device which can either break or fail at the most inopportune time.

This Sitka blacktail deer required a tricky downhill shot from 45 yards. However, the author's pre-season practice made the shot entirely subconscious.

Also, some of today's angle-compensating rangefinders may not be as accurate as you assume. Most are set for specific arrow speed, and that may not be the same as yours. With that in mind, let's explore the art of using an inclinometer and cut chart.

Using an Inclinometer and Cut Chart: A great inclinometer designed specifically for the bowhunter in mind is the Slope-Shot II **www.getoat.com**. It costs about $25 and is effective, since it can be mounted to your laser rangefinder, and as you sight the rangefinder on target, you simply press the "hold" button on the inclinometer, then take the rangefinder away from your eye and instantly you have the measured shooting angle.

M	Cut-Chart Archery Combined – Angle To Target																				
	0°		15°		20°		25°		30°		35°		40°		45°		50°		55°		60°
Yards / Meters To Target	U	D	U	D	U	D	U	D	U	D	U	D	U	D	U	D	U	D	U	D	U
20			19	19	18	18	17	16	15	14	xx	xx	xx	xx	xx	xx	xx	xx	xx	xx	xx
25			24	24	23	23	22	22	21	20	19	18	16	15	xx	xx	xx	xx	xx	xx	xx
30			29	29	28	28	27	26	25	25	24	23	21	20	19	17	14	xx	xx	xx	xx
35			34	33	33	32	32	31	30	29	28	27	26	25	23	22	20	18	15	xx	xx
40			39	38	38	37	36	35	35	33	33	31	30	29	27	26	24	22	20	18	xx
45			44	43	43	42	41	40	39	38	37	35	34	33	31	29	28	26	24	22	19
50			49	48	47	46	46	44	44	42	41	39	38	36	35	33	31	29	27	25	22
55			54	52	52	51	51	49	48	46	46	43	43	40	39	37	35	33	31	28	26
60			59	57	57	55	56	53	53	50	50	47	47	44	43	40	39	36	34	31	29
65			64	62	62	60	60	57	58	55	55	51	51	48	47	43	42	39	37	34	32
70			69	67	67	64	65	62	62	59	59	55	55	51	51	47	46	42	41	37	35

A cut chart, such as this one offered by Slope-Shot *www.getoat.com*, simply tells you how much yardage to "take off" from the shot distance for a given angle. This allows you to make precise hits.

With this information, you reference your "cut" chart, which comes with the Slope-Shot II, or is available for free at the manufacturer's Web site. A cut chart is a simple reference that tells you what distance to aim for based on the shot angle and line-of-sight distance. In every instance, the real shooting distance is a subtraction from the line-of-sight distance, or what your regular rangefinder reads. The cut chart included with the Slope-Shot is based on a 400-grain arrow shooting 250 fps, which proves accurate within plus or minus 1-yard for even set-ups that vary by 60 grains and 40 fps. However, you can purchase a custom chart for your specific arrow weight and speed at a small cost, usually about $8. The chart

40 yd.

50 yd.

30 yd.

Extreme up or downhill shots are possible, but only if you aim precisely for the horizontal distance. For example, this illustration shows how the line-of-sight distance can vary greatly from horizontal shooting distance. In this case, you should aim at the buck using your 30-yard pin, not your 50.

features angles and distances in 5-degree/yard increments up to 60 degrees and 70 yards. You should also know that there are slight variances in uphill or downhill-shooting distances, as noted on the cut chart.

The chart is sized so you can tape it to a 3 x 5 index card or to your rangefinder or bow limb using rugged, weather-proof clear packaging tape.

Using this system, let's say you have a mule deer standing sharply below you. Your range-finder reads 40 yards to the big buck, and your inclinometer reads 35 degrees. Now cross-reference this information with your cut chart. It will tell you to shoot for 32.8 yards for a dead-on strike to the vitals.

Randy Ulmer practices with his inclinometer constantly during a hunt; that way, when he's stalking an animal, he already has a good idea of the shooting angle. From here, he simply uses his standard laser rangefinder and subtracts a certain percentage from the distance, based on the estimated shot angle. "If the animal is on a 25-degree slope, then I know I have to take off 10 percent from the shot distance," he told me. This procedure allows him to execute the shot faster without creating extra motion to look at an inclinometer and cut chart while he's pinned down close to a wary buck or bull.

Regardless of the method you use, include extreme uphill and downhill shooting in your regular practice. To make these shots count, you'll still need to rely on good shooting form, which means maintaining good torso posture. A quick and effective way to do this is to draw your bow from a level position, then twist downward at the waist, doing your best to keep your torso relatively straight.

Sidehill Shots

This is where a sight with a good bubble level comes in handy. When standing on a slope, it's most natural to lean the top bow limb away from the hill, but to maintain horizontal accuracy, you must lean the limb toward the hill.

A precisely mounted bowsight level will tell you how to position your bow perfectly plump to make these shots count. However, the level must be just that, precise. Bowsights with second and third-axis adjustability allow for the greatest amount of accuracy. The third-axis feature compensates for off-camber, uphill or downhill shooting, while the second-axis works effectively only for flat-ground shooting.

Rarely are we faced with level shots in the field, particularly on Western game.

Fact: When standing on a slope, your bow's limb must lean into the hill for proper horizontal accuracy.

Again, it's important to practice shots like these well before you find yourself standing on a side hill with a big buck out in front of you. You'll notice an awkward feel in your shooting stance while taking these shots. In most cases, it's best to bend your knees and spread your feet apart as necessary to maintain a firm stance. Shooting with feet close together can disrupt proper upper body shooting posture, which will cause accuracy issues.

Shooting in the Wind

I remember shooting in one 3-D tournament that was nearly ruined by severe high winds. While some of the best shooters walked off the course—to protect their good shooting habits—I bit my tongue and continued to shoot in the blazing gusts, because I wanted to practice under the same harsh conditions I sometimes find myself in the field.

Overall it was not fun, but I learned several valuable lessons that day. For starters, I believe windy-day shooting with a quiver on your bow increases shooting difficulty two-fold, and using back-tension to trigger the shot becomes much more difficult. I also recognized that

BY JOE BELL

high wind speed is very inconsistent. This means calculating your arrow's expected wind drift for a given wind is quite like guessing what poker hand you'll have before the cards are dealt.

This was my analysis at the end of the day. In high winds (40-to-50 mph), shooting at a big-game animal beyond 35 yards is hopeless, if not unethical. When the wind gusts are this high, they tend to buck more than remain a constant current of air. This can force your aim and arrow in the wrong place at the wrong time.

This means calculating your arrow's predicted amount of wind drift can be difficult. Some archers practice with a wind gauge and come up with their own particular wind-drift chart, much as a cut chart used for angled shots.

Some have tried other methods, such as tossing blades of grass at waist level and predicting the wind speed based on the travel of the grass. All these methods work, but you must spend an awful lot of time preparing your own arrow's wind-drift chart.

My friend, Ron Way, is an aerospace engineer. According to Ron, as arrows fly through the brisk wind, they tend to fishtail or corkscrew. The arrows naturally want to follow the path of least resistance, which is into the wind. This can cause arrows to easily be misguided, especially with fixed-blade heads. When the wind is extremely strong, arrows can fishtail severely, which can cause jackknife-style mechanical heads to cartwheel harshly on impact.

Also, keep in mind, the less surface area your arrow shaft has the less it will drift in the wind. For example, small-diameter shafts and short, low-profile fletching creates less surface area, both which buck the wind better. Heavier shafts also drift less, given the shaft diameter and length are the same.

Fact: Shooting at animals in moderate wind is doable; however, if the wind is bucking hard it is likely unethical.

When practicing on windy days, I wouldn't overdo it. Wind can cause irregular aiming habits, but some practice is vital to your success.

"I force myself to practice in the wind," says Ulmer. "So I have a real good idea of what my arrows do. I was on a hunt in eastern Colorado. The wind was blowing very hard, and I missed a shot at a deer—not by a few inches, but by a few feet! I felt irresponsible for having taken such a marginal shot. I was completely unprepared. I told myself that would never happen again. So immediately I began shooting at some round hay bales in the big fields near camp. In due time I became familiar with my arrow's flight path in the wind. For example, at 40 yards, in a very strong wind, I'd aim 4 feet to the side and hit dead center." On that hunt, Ulmer ended up shooting a monster mule deer, even though the wind was blowing fiercely at the time.

While shooting in the wind, archers can use two aiming techniques to counter arrow drift. The first and most obvious method is to simply aim off target a sustained amount. The second is to use your bubble level on your sight. By aiming a "half-bubble" or a "full bubble" out of center, you can correct for wind drift.

Both methods work well, given the archer practices a lot. Many great shots I know prefer to aim using the bubble method. Most say it gives them more of a mental edge since the sight pin is still on target, instead of suspended in thin air. Experiment to see what works best for you.

Ulmer prefers to hold off target. "I don't use the bubble method," he said. "There is not enough 'room' in the bubble for strong winds and each bubble is different. I would have to reuse the same bubble forever."

The author credits relentless practice on moving targets, particularly small game, for his successful shot on this walking caribou.

"I don't have a specific method I use to gauge wind… I guess through hours and hours of practicing at long range I have developed a feel for how far to hold off or bubble in order to make a shot," says Darin Cooper. "I prefer to bubble the bow unless the wind is significant. On targets I aim better if I can put the pin in the center because my pin seems to be drawn there so it seems more difficult to aim off. However, with my hunting arrow setup (3.6-inch vanes and fixed-blade broadheads) the wind drift is about four times what I see with Easton X-10s shooting target. Therefore, at longer ranges bubbling over is usually not enough. I don't have a problem picking a spot and holding there while aiming at animals or 3-D targets."

Obstacles and Arrow Trajectory

Drawing while you're flat to the ground may seem a little extreme, but it is often necessary when stalking open country animals where it's often hard to draw your bow without being detected.

In the fading evening light a bull elk responded to my seductive cow mews. Dashing for another 100 yards, I quickly set up in a natural meadow, outlined by chest-high evergreens.

Planting myself behind one of these saplings for cover, I blew a few more times to seal the deal, and seconds later the bull emerged like a ghost from the eerie shadows.

He silently marched across the open grass, looking in every direction. Now standing 20 yards away, looking as big as a barn door and completely broadside, it was the moment to shoot. But, a problem quickly arose. In the heat of the moment, I failed to look over my makeshift blind—my shooting tunnel was almost covered with suspended branches and pine needles. Knowing the tiny openings were only two feet from my bow, I quickly analyzed my arrow's flight path and somehow just knew the arrow would fill one of the gaps, even though my 20-yard pin would be partially covered by the tree.

Fact: Shooting under, over or through obstacles is part of being a versatile bowhunting shot.

Be sure to practice angled shots using a 3-D target, preferably one that identifies the location of a deer's vitals, such as this one offered by Rinehart.

Inching to full draw as slowly as possible, the bull snapped his head in my direction, obviously capturing the movement. But it was too late; the arrow flashed ahead and into the lower third of his chest. As the arrow struck, I still vividly remember a couple of the pine needles dancing about.

Over the years, I'd say almost 50 percent of my shots taken in the field involved some kind of natural barrier I had to shoot through, around or below. Without prior shot practice, you'll either fumble these relatively easy shots or lack the confidence to even take them. Either way, the quarry gets away.

The good news is these shots are pretty simplistic in nature. Simply hold up your un-drawn bow, aim with the appropriate sight pin, and determine if your arrow will collide with the barrier. It's that easy.

For example, take a deer that is 35 yards away. You want to shoot at this buck, but you quickly notice an intervening tree limb, which you determine is 23 yards away. By lifting your bow and fixing your 30-yard pin on the buck's vitals, you can determine if your 20-yard pin is close enough to the limb that your arrow will collide with it. If it doesn't appear a crash is imminent, then you can aim with confidence that your arrow will pass above or below the tree branch. The key is to know this and react quickly. If not, in a hunting situation your opportunity will rapidly fade away.

Shooting through or around foliage that is close in front of you, which was the case with my shot on the elk, calls for other considerations. As the arrow moves out of the bow, it starts well below your line of sight, 7 inches or more. Archers with low anchor points notice this even more. In other words, the arrow doesn't cross anywhere near your wad of sight pins until it travels 5 yards or more from the bow. Be sure to practice at ultra-close distances, as your arrows rise at given distances. This will allow you to know when it is safe for you to shoot through narrow windows in the brush.

Moving Shots

Some animals aren't prone to standstill, even if you try to whistle at them. Caribou are one of the best examples. My first trip to Northwest Territories to hunt central barren-ground caribou is a perfect illustration.

After four days of hunting, the only caribou I could find not running was one bedded not far from a lakeshore. After an hour I realized I couldn't get close enough for a shot. So I waited along the lake's shoreline and shot him as he got up and trotted past me. I had practiced similar shots all summer long on small game near my house, so I placed the sight pin out in front of the animal's shoulders simply by feel and made a solid chest hit.

On that same trip I shot my second caribou as it nonchalantly walked across a large opening, leaving me no choice but to take aim and fire. If I had hesitated or refused to shoot under such conditions, I'm certain I would've gone home empty-handed.

Fact: Roll a tire and shoot through it; it will teach you about sustained leads on close-range moving shots.

When shooting downhill, be sure to maintain correct shooting posture. This shooter's torso remains straight, despite the shooting angle. This photo shows pro shooter John Dudley in action.

Clearly, moving game represents an expert's target. Without intense practice, these shots are very inadvisable. Also, resist taking such shots unless the buck or bull is walking at a slow pace and is less than 20 yards away.

Besides shooting at running small game, a great way to practice moving shots is to take an old tire and shoot at it while it's rolling at various speeds. You'll need a friend to assist you with this, and it's recommended that you use rubber blunt-tipped arrows to prevent ricochets. Such practice will help you identify the required aim, or lead in this case, necessary to pass your arrow through the tire.

You can also use a 3-D target mounted to a pulley and cable line, which creates a fast-moving target.

Chapter 11
Delivering at the Moment of Truth

Staying Mentally Tough at Crunch Time

"What this power is I cannot say; all I know is that it exists and it becomes available only when a man is in that state of mind in which he knows exactly what he wants and is fully determined not to quit until he finds it."
—Alexander Graham Bell

Every bowhunter gets excited in the face of a trophy. The key is to manage this excitement by thinking about every step of the shot, just like you do on the range.

My friends and I called him Big Jim, because he was clearly one of the biggest Southern California mule deer we'd ever seen loping the coastal mountain range.

I had a fascination with this buck to the deepest extent. Weekend after weekend, I'd trek the rugged, brushy slopes searching for this buck. On one occasion, I spotted him vacating a canyon area and I ran for more than a mile with my pack and heavy boots, trying to intercept the giant 4 x 4 buck. And I did, only the shot was much too far.

One day, I left the office a little early and got to my hunting area on time. My boss was fully aware of my obsession for this buck.

I knew of a deep, nasty canyon filled with brush where a spring jutted from the ground. I set up on a fairly open hillside 100 yards above it, and then waited in the hot, August sun.

About 1 1/2 hours before dark, I noticed a doe coming out of the God-forsaken ravine. I quickly became excited, but then relaxed a bit knowing it was only a doe. But like a mirage, his giant antler beams jutted from the foliage. There he was—my Big Jim—nosing, pushing the doe up the gnarly, 40-degree slope.

I waited for a shot, almost shaking. Little by little the twosome got closer, as the monster continued his harassment. Over, around, and even through bushes they went. Before I knew it, the doe was just below and climbing upward. She popped out of cover about 35 yards away.

I knew the shot would come to fruition—it would soon be my golden chance at this legendary buck. Knowing full well he'd appear in seconds, my nerves became increasingly tangled. Emotions were now in full flow.

At full draw in a flash, I held for the moment I so longed for. Despite my physical strength, mentally I couldn't draw a good bead on the buck's vitals; my focus was obviously on his wide-sweeping 26-some-inch beams. Uncomfortable, feeling physically awkward as I held for nearly a minute, I frantically whipped my sight on his chest and released. The arrow flew hair-lengths below his armpit. Even today, it stands as the worst bowhunting moment in my life.

The interesting part of all this is during this phase in my archery career, I could place arrow after arrow in a tight cluster on a 60-yard butt. I had successfully shot other deer at ranges beyond 50 yards. And nearly every other weekend I had drilled one ground squirrel and rabbit after another at challenging distances. I thought I was ready for Big Jim, and so did my friends.

Yet "buck fever" had the power to heighten every nerve in my body, all at the worst possible time.

Feeling excited is natural under intense encounters with big game. The problem is, high excitement will plague your shooting. Controlling this emotional element is crucial in executing a good shot. Here are some helpful tips on how to overcome or at least manage this common bowhunting ailment.

Practice with Pressure in Mind

Certain things stick with you, and I remember an old friend telling me, "You'll shoot (at big game) like you practice." Simple but poignantly true. To expect to perform better on big game than on targets is absurd. A steady, accurate shot in the woods only comes from executing *perfect, perfect* shots on the range.

Fact: To control excitement, keep your mind preoccupied with all the steps necessary to make a great shot.

Consistent bowhunting success doesn't just happen. To make high-pressure shots again and again, you must have a system in place, such as a mental drill you go through just prior to hitting full draw.

When practicing, allow each shot to absorb you; focus on each step *(Chapter 1)*, and just before drawing the bow, visualize the perfect shot. Practice this enough and simply allow "auto pilot" to take over when the chips are down. Chances are, you'll do it right just like you have so many times before, and the odds will be leaning on your side.

But, please don't take this process light-heartedly. You can't ingrain it one day and leave it out the next. Nor can you learn it in the couple of weeks before opening day. Carry it out throughout the spring and summer so it becomes a customary habit, like the mindless act of inscribing your signature on a check.

Pick a Spot!

The author remembers feeling a strong dose of buck fever while drawing down on this Wyoming whitetail. His saving grace was aiming intensely at where he wanted to hit, which seemed to force a good shot.

In the heat of the moment, most bowhunters fail to do it, despite it being so elementary. When you're about to pull back on a trophy, taking a gander at the lower one-third part of the chest, where you want your arrow to strike, just isn't refined enough to counter a less-than-perfect aim. In practice, if you were to aim at this large of a target, you'd scatter arrows all over, every time.

Precise aiming equals precise arrow impact, particularly when your breathing is elevated and your sights could be trembling in a giant 2-inch circle. Pick out the smallest patch of hair or crease on the animal's vital zone and start performing some serious tunnel vision. This is your only objective at this point…until your arrow splits this mark.

This kind of focusing has a way of poising your excitement so you can perform as a shooter.

"I find I do best when I think of only one thing, and for me it is 'pick a spot,' " says Mike Slinkard, pro shooter, accomplished bowhunter, and president and owner of Winner's Choice Bowstrings. "I just keep mentally repeating this in the moment just before and during the shot. I find this helps control my nerves…ones that will make even an easy shot impossible.

 "If there is time I will quickly picture the shot happening perfectly in my mind (just as I do when shooting a target archery shot)," says Slinkard. "All this happens very quickly, and again it's really about controlling emotion more than anything. As far as the shot itself, that will just happen subconsciously as it does in practice."

Have a Hunting Pre-Shot Checklist

When mentally preparing himself for the shot, Randy Ulmer likes to preoccupy his mind with certain variables, such as shot angle, exact shooting distance, when to draw, for example. This helps him combat buck fever, he says.

Before shooting at an animal, develop a mental checklist, similar to the kind of routine the top experts use. Well-known bowhunters Randy Ulmer and Chuck Adams have good ones.

"My checklist has evolved over the years," says Ulmer. "If I know a shot is eminent, I start to focus my mind on certain variables…this helps me combat buck fever. I try not to do anything without thinking about it first."

TECH TIPS

After the Shot

Take several deep breaths, stay put, then observe *exactly* what just happened. If you didn't see the animal go down, note specifically where the animal was standing at arrow impact, how it reacted seconds after the hit, and where it ran. Retrace the flight and impact of the arrow. Did it find the mark, or was it slightly off? Recognize as many details as possible at this moment, all which may come in handy if you have some tedious blood trailing on your hands. Do not move until you've taken inventory of all this, then and only then, clearly mark where you were standing at the shot. Then, walk a straight line to the hit site. Upon arrival, mark it as well.

Now's the time to start looking for signs of blood—some or a lot should be present. Keep a strong eye out for the arrow, or parts of it. Keep in mind, often times, blood doesn't start spewing or dropping out of the animal until he runs a few yards after the hit.

Ulmer's Pre-Shot Checklist:

1. Examine Shot Angle (Mostly applies to mule deer and sheep hunting). As an example, if he estimates the animal is on a 25-degree slope, he knows to take off 10 percent from the shot distance.

2. Establish Exact Shot Distance (Ulmer wants to put his pin exactly where it needs to be for a perfect shot, not a close-enough hit.)

3. Examine Arrow Flight Path (Possible interferences like tree limbs, etc.)

4. Determine that I am using the right pin in exactly the right place.

5. Patience…Patience (His mantra—Patience seldom goes un-rewarded)

6. Aim…Aim…Aim…Until the Shot Breaks

Adams' Pre-Shot Checklist:

1. Is the Shot Clear? Overview of possible obstacles. Visualize arrow's path when necessary

2. Angle of Shot—Compensate accordingly (Adams has carried an angle meter with him for about three decades)

3. Get the Range (If time, use laser rangefinder; if not he eyes the distance as best as possible

4. Pick a spot

5. Point the bow straight at the target, pull straight back

6. Relax bow hand as much as possible

7. Take the first good high-percentage shot

Chuck Adams believes in taking the first good, high-percentage shot that comes his way. He says a lot of bowhunters tend to wait for the very best shot in the world, which rarely happens.

How to Gain Confidence

Following your checklist during the moment of truth won't be enough. You'll have to put it into practice well before this moment…over and over again. Stump-shooting, small-game hunting, and 3-D tournaments are the perfect places for refining your execution.

I like combining all three since each has qualities to offer. Stump-shooting and small-game hunting allow you to "suit up" just like you do on a big-game outing. When hunting small game you are out stalking and/or ambushing, just like you would a buck or bull. You use camo duds for concealment, binocular to enhance visibility, and a rangefinder for accurate shooting distance. You're essentially big-game hunting, only the target is smaller.

Fact: Picking a spot and focusing on that spot is the most powerful medicine against buck fever.

Three-D shoots, though different from hunting, bring on pressure variables that are beneficial. Small crowds of people watching you shoot can create nervousness and this is just what you want. If you can master shooting "under the gun," chances are you'll do well at combating buck fever.

Visualization practice is very helpful as well.

During practice sessions, Slinkard practices a lot of visualization, imagining a real shot on a live animal. "The interesting thing is that your subconscious mind—for all of its strengths—cannot tell the difference between reality and vividly imagined events," said Slinkard. "So by actively practicing while vividly imaging performing well under the stresses of a hunting situation it is possible to actually gain 'simulated' high-stress hunting experience. When the real-life shot occurs, the subconscious mind thinks that it is just something it does all the time, and stress levels and corresponding mistakes fall dramatically."

With this technique, Slinkard says it's important to visualize some things not working out either, such as the animal moving too fast for a shot, presenting the wrong angle or spooking. This way, it's much like reality in the hunting woods. Shots don't always work out, so you want to visualize that as well, and eventually move on to other images where it does.

TECH TIPS

Blood Trailing Tips

The way I see it, you can make blood trailing as complicated as you want, but it's rather simple. If you feel like you've made a solid chest shot through both lungs and you've got bright, frothy blood on the ground and/or your arrow to prove it, wait 30-to-40 minutes and start trailing. You'll soon find your trophy.

If not, you must wait, sometimes for a very long time. Patience is the key to recovering animals when shots are less than ideal. How long you wait depends on certain factors. Here are five common situations that I often see.

Situation No.1: If you feel you've made a good shot, but don't have any blood to show for it, err on the side of caution and wait *at least one hour.* Realize broadhead holes can "seal up" because of fatty tissue, which causes massive internal bleeding. Despite little to no blood trail, the animal won't go far. To the very best of your ability, follow what fresh sign is available (mainly tracks), searching for the smallest specks of blood. If this proves futile, begin grid-searching (walking each section of the woods systematically) looking for your fallen trophy.

Situation No. 2: If you sense a high or very low hit, and note the blood on the arrow or ground is bright red with no bubbles in it, there's a good chance the broadhead caused nothing more than a flesh wound. Follow the blood as far as you can. A common trait of superficial, flesh wounds is a plentiful initial blood trail which progresses down to tiny specks that eventually peters out, usually after about 200-to-300 yards or so.

Situation No. 3: If you feel like the arrow struck "far back" in the mid section (guts), wait at least 6 hours before trailing the deer. Pushing gut-shot deer is a very common mistake (I hear about it year after year), but what a huge mistake it is. A gut-shot deer or elk is capable of moving quite quickly if pushed, and the adrenaline of the chase could push it for miles. Once that happens, your chances of finding it are exponentially zero since arrows bisecting intestines or paunch rarely leave much blood. Not pushed, gut-shot deer usually bed down within 100-to-200 yards from where the shot occurred, expiring after several hours for easy recovery.

Situation No. 4: If a marginal shot occurs, and the animal is still in sight, possibly hunched up from the shot and unaware of what happened, do all you can to sneak in for a follow-up shot. No matter what you do, don't let the animal see you, which could cause it to run frantically. This works mainly in open or semi-open terrain. Dense, noisy terrain could foil any attempts at closing the gap, and waiting is a better plan. However, do your best to monitor the animal's travel, staying just close enough to see its whereabouts.

Situation No. 5: In a rain or snowstorm, follow the blood trail immediately, but only if you suspect a solid chest hit. Otherwise, always wait. Pushing marginally wounded game is a mistake, no matter the circumstance.

When to Shoot

Participating in 3-D matches will help you shoot better on big game.

Shots at big game are precious for most of us—you may only get one chance during a long hunt. When that chance comes, it's important to recognize it. Interestingly enough, a lot of bowhunters fail miserably in this department. A whole lot of factors come into play that will define the right time to shoot. Animal behavior, shot angle, and personal shooting comfort are the key factors. However, the key, in my opinion, is to recognize the first *good* opportunity, not the very best one in the world.

A lot of guys are looking for those hallmark chances—an animal at 20 yards, relaxed, perfectly broadside or slightly quartering away—a gimme shot, really. That's great, mind you, but the reality of it is that this kind of shot may never come during a week's hunt. You may have to settle for a more challenging but certainly doable shot, like a buck standing 37-yards away with its vitals only exposed through a 12-inch circle in the brush.

Don't take me wrong, now. By no means am I advocating unethical shots on game (desperation shots are for fools), but if you've practiced like a madman all spring and summer long, and you know your arrow's flight trajectory inside and out and confidence is reigning, I say take the shot. Don't mess around.

"I take the first good high percentage shot within my

Only you can determine when the right time is to shoot, and we must strive for ethical shots at all times. The author was able to slip within the outer limits of his comfortable shooting range on this Colorado buck. Mentally he felt confident in making the shot, so he didn't hesitate in coming to full draw.

killing/confidence level," says Chuck Adams. "A lot of bowhunters tend to dawdle when faced with animals within their effective range, waiting for the best shot in the world. In the end, they go home empty-handed."

A few seasons back, I stalked three nice mule deer bucks, all 4 x 4s with 26-to-28-inch spreads. The deer were feeding in the open with nothing but pine needles and a few scraggly bushes separating us. When the moment was right, I crawled a bit closer and got within the outer edge of my personal effective range. It was a pretty long shot, but I knew I could make it. I knew, because I had no lingering doubts; that's your "green light" go ahead.

From there, I went into proactive mode. Once the first deer disappeared in a cut in the terrain, I hit full draw. I tracked the second deer but it too dropped out of sight. When the third and smallest buck stopped momentarily, the shot was off and the arrow made a resounding thump. Later that day, as I was packing out deer quarters, it was obvious I made the right decision.

> ### TECH TIPS
>
> ## Shoot Does!
>
> Real shooting practice is the best fix to minimize buck fever. Hunting does or other plentiful big game (such as wild boar or exotics) is a helpful tool. In most cases, these animals create nearly as much excitement during the shot execution, and familiarizing yourself with such encounters will teach you how to personally deal with this kind of rush. You can practice breathing routines, your personal mental checklist, shot visualization, and other strategies. If you miss a shot because of over excitement, and you probably will, rejection isn't so costly. You'll soon forget about your miss on one of these critters, but a big buck you won't. By hunting does and other plentiful big game animals, you'll eventually come up with the right techniques that help calm your nerves. The key is a lot of practice. Personally, nothing heightens my confidence levels more than this kind of hunting.

In that example I could've done many things differently. I could have been more patient, waiting for the deer to possibly get closer—you know, for that slam-dunk opportunity. Or, I could have waited for any of the bucks to reappear again, hoping they'd calmly graze once more, so I could shoot at a motionless 3-D-like target. Yes, I could've, but no guarantees exist in any of that. Why gamble when a good shot opportunity was already before me?

Experience is the true indicator of what constitutes a good or bad shot for you. However, after years of bowhunting, my advice is this: be as proactive as possible when animals are within your effective range. Think but be ready to react quickly. There's a fine line between all this. Exercising patience is crucial; if there's any doubt about the shot angle, don't shoot. The last thing you want to do is ruin a potentially great shot opportunity by forcing things and shooting at the wrong time, perhaps causing a superficial wound or a lengthy blood trail that begins but leaves you going home empty-handed.

"I think inexperienced bowhunters often rush the shot," says Ulmer. "They're so excited to finally get a shot that they want it over with. They are afraid the deer is going to get away. If they would take an additional 10 seconds they would shoot more deer—an occasional buck would get away, but in the long run they'd have more success. You usually have more time than you think to execute the shot."

If there's a time to slow down, it should be during the shot phase. Focus on the steps of the shot and carry them through. As was stated earlier, this will help you keep your cool.

When to Draw

A lot of bowhunters fail to draw at the right time, and usually get busted doing it. It's better to foresee where an animal will appear, come to full draw, and then wait for the opportunity to arrive.

If the shot's a go, the next step is to get drawn, unseen. This is a huge battle in most situations, and again, many bowhunters do it wrong.

Mistake No. 1 is drawing within view of the animal's eyes. The sharp eyes of a bull or buck will catch such movement every time. Wait until the animal's eyes are obscured by a tree, bush or rock, then hit full draw.

Mistake No. 2 is not drawing early enough into the encounter. When an animal is too far for a shot, but is moving in your direction and you predict a likely shot encounter, now is the time to get to full draw. Most bowhunters seem to want to wait until the animal is in the wide open before placing the rangefinder on the animal, then coming to full draw. This works only some of the times, given the animal turns his head so you can draw undetected. But most of the time, the animal never turns, and in this case, drawing your bow is impossible without being seen.

Fact: Visualize the perfect shot before attempting to take one. By doing so, you increase the chances of it becoming a reality.

In cases like these, predict where the animal is likely to travel, pre-determine shooting distances to these windows using your rangefinder, and be ready to strike—that means waiting at full draw as the animal pops into view. I can't emphasize this enough. This is all part of recognizing a *good,* high-percentage shot.

Here's a great example. A few seasons back, while hunting Sitka blacktail deer on Kodiak Island, Alaska, I spotted a group of deer grazing along a snow-covered slope. Noticing there were three decent bucks in the bunch, I stalked in from below, totally hidden by snow and brush. However, as I eased upward, I could see the tops of the deer, including one good branch-antlered buck.

Instantly, I figured the distance by placing the rangefinder on his polished horns, and drew my bow. I walked up the hill five more yards before the snow bank was clear of his chest. At the very instant the buck snapped his head in my direction, the arrow was on its way.

Maneuvering until I had a clear shot on that buck, then drawing my bow, would have proved to be a huge mistake in this case. The deer would've surely caught my movement and likely bolted, ruining the shot opportunity all together.

Sizing Up Ethical Shots

As far as I'm concerned, if you take anything other than broadside or slightly quartering-away shots on big game, you're flirting with being unethical. There could be a few rare exceptions to this, but not many.

Let's explore the details of ethical shots and perhaps some exceptions to this rule.

Anytime an animal is standing perfectly broadside or at a slight quartering-away position, its vital organs are unobstructed by heavy bones, allowing the best possible access and penetration for the arrow and broadhead to bisect both lungs, which expires the animal quickly. This is the goal in effective bowhunting: to hit the animal through both lungs.

The perfect aiming spot on a broadside deer is the point four inches up and inline with the knuckle on the leg (right where it meets the brisket). With a slight quartering-away deer, come up the same amount from its brisket, but horizontally align your

TECH TIPS

Be Rangefinder Ready

Most bowhunters carry their rangefinder in a belt pouch with a zippered or button closure. This is fine, however, if you anticipate a shooting opportunity, be sure to open the case fully, so access is as easy as a one-hand grab (you'll probably need your other hand to hold your bow).

Also, keep in mind that most belt cases supplied with rangefinders are often too noisy and too snug fitting for serious field use. For this reason, purchase a quieter, roomier case so extraction of the unit is super simple and dropping it back into the case is just as fumble free. This way you can focus on making a good shot.

I prefer a fleece case with a flap closure and quick-release buckle (such as the one offered by Day One Camouflage). By carefully pinching the buckle, I can open the case quietly.

However, most of the time I prefer to sling my rangefinder around my neck; it's much faster to use this way, and hand (body) movement is greatly minimized. I fashion a heavy fleece strap to the unit to reduce noise and to increase comfort, and adjust the length of it so the rangefinder rides just above my binocular. Here, I can one-hand grab the rangefinder, get the shooting distance, and drop it back in place so I can prepare for the shot—all in a near blink of an eye.

"A man of sense is never discouraged by difficulties; he redoubles his industry and his diligence, he perseveres, and infallibly prevails at last."

—Lord Chesterfield

sight pin with the offside leg. Either of these shots allows for maximum margin of arrow placement to the vital organs, which includes the lungs and heart.

Beyond this, things become dicey as the vitals are covered by heavy bone and tissue, which can cause all kinds of penetration and deflection issues.

One of the most tempting shots is the quartering-to shot, but it's a huge mistake. In this position, the animal's shoulder and leg bones cover most of the lung/heart region, except for that rear portion of the onside lung and possibly the liver (given it's on the animal's right side). To catch this single lung, your arrow must hit perfectly one-third of the way up the chest cavity, barely nick the edge of the shoulder blade, where it will bisect this 3-inch portion or so of the lung, then bury itself into stomach and intestines. With this hit, the animal will eventually die, but its death will come through slow, arduous infection. This does not constitute a good shot, even if you happen to hit the animal perfectly.

Straight-on shots become dicey as well, though some experts will take these shots under certain criteria. For example, I've seen a lot of pronghorn antelope shot more or less straight on as they drank at a watering hole. With moderately thin bones, penetration on these animals is not much of a problem given your bow generates more than 55 foot-pounds of kinetic energy.

Randy Ulmer (a veterinarian) had this to say about straight-on shots. "I have never taken this kind of shot and never will. It's better to be patient. Your chances of killing that bull are 1 in 10, and the same goes for a deer. You are basically shooting for the thoracic inlet. It's a hole about the size of your fist, but where is it? You don't really know."

Chuck Adams says he would take such shots, but only under certain circumstances.

"On a big-boned animal like an elk, I would not," said Adams. "For shots like that, two factors become important: Size of the animal and temperament of the animal. I've never taken a shot at a whitetail deer straight on because you know they'll jump the string. On the other hand, I shot my formal world record Sitka Blacktail deer back in 1986 with a full frontal shot from 35 yards. I knew from past experience these deer are not notorious for jumping the string. I also knew my powerful bow/arrow would shoot straight through the brisket bone and into the vitals. However, if you wait, you'll usually get the broadside shot you need in."

As far as I'm concerned, all other shots at big game are to be avoided—period. To intentionally shoot an animal in the mid-section (guts) or through the rear end (ham or anus) is purely immoral and leaves way too much to chance. The odds of dispatching that animal quickly are slim to none, whereas the chance of gimping the animal or causing slow, painful death is extremely high.

Fact: Ethical bowhunting means shooting an arrow through *both* the animal's lungs for a clean, rapid kill.

Chapter 12
Bow Maintenance: Fixing It All

Become the Pro Shop Tech

"One of the rarest things that a man ever does, is to do the best he can."
—*Josh Billings*

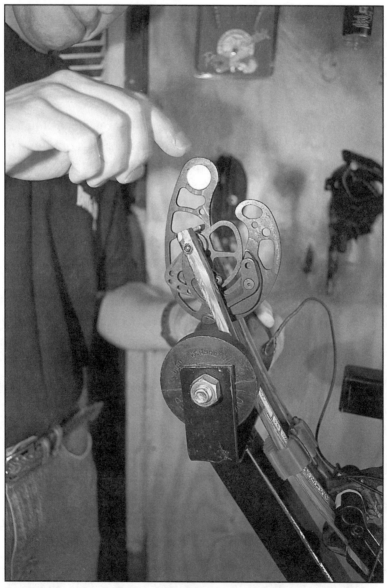

If your bow's cams use plastic-composite bushings, be sure to check them for wear regularly. It's usually best to replace bushings each time you change out bowstrings. A worn bushing can create accuracy problems.

BY JOE BELL

Each year I see it time and time again—bows that need work at the worst possible time, often just before a big hunting trip or actually even during one. Just last September in elk camp, I saw several bows that were clearly out of whack. Arrow rests with slipping/non-served pull-down cords, fractured center servings, loose and/or damaged fletching, cams that were out of alignment, and creeping bowstrings were just a few of the problems that stood out. In each case, I was told that they thought their buddy at the pro shop had taken care of everything and that the bow was in good order.

Before I go further, let me say this: a reputable pro shop is great, but you cannot count on it to be your saving grace when you're nearly out the door to go hunting or to shoot a 3-D match and, suddenly, you've just found yourself with a broken or poor functioning bow. This is the prime reason why I prefer to do my own bow repairs. But there are other great reasons for knowing bow maintenance as well, such as lower repair costs, a finer tuned bow, and becoming intimately familiar with a bow's functional attributes. In the end, you'll become a better, more confident shot, because you will know your bow is set up as good as it can possibly be.

Fact: A quality bow press is vital to home bow repair.

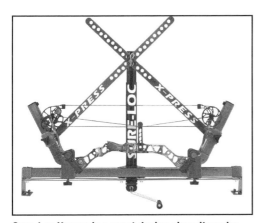

Sure-Loc Xpress is a great design since it works by placing downward pressure on the bow's limbs, not the riser.

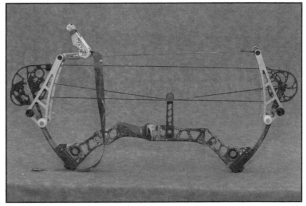

A portable press is useful when traveling. This is the Ratchet Press by Ram Products. The author considers it the most versatile, easy-to-use portable press on the market.

Tools of the Trade

Before you can fix your bow's various problems, you will need all of the right tools. It is in your best interest to invest in the highest quality gear that you can afford from the get go. It will pay off for you by way of easy function and long-lasting performance.

The most important tool for you to have, in my opinion, is a sturdy bow press. Nothing in my workshop gets used as much as my press. The bowstrings are the lifeblood of your set-up and you can't remove and repair them without a press to relax the bow's limbs.

I don't recommend portable models for regular home bow maintenance. A serious bow mechanic constantly depresses bows, and a compact-size press makes this chore kind of a tiring hassle. A full-size press is safer, too.

Apple, Big-Squeeze, Sure-Loc, and others make high-quality bench bow presses. I like the Big Squeeze, since it works so easily with every style of bow, particularly the extreme-parallel limb bows of today.

Note: When pressing a bow, insist on placing the downward pressure at the very ends of the riser points, or along the base of the limbs where they meet the limb pockets. Also, always unscrew the limb bolts 6 turns from the very most bottom position. The less pressure you put on your bow's riser, the better. Bow risers will bend, and even the slightest bend will wreck the bow's accuracy potential.

Fact: By building your own arrows, you can repair them easily and maintain a level of quality control, which will increase shooting consistency.

Other critical tools include a T-square, center-serving tool(s), wheel-spacer kit, axle lube, clamp-on nocksets and nocking plier (if necessary), D-loop material, string wax, and various types of serving material.

TECH TIPS

Identifying String Creep

String creep is the No. 1 enemy of your set-up. To easily identify this important variable and to fix it promptly you must retain knowledge of your bow's axle-to-axle length, brace height, arrow-length to riser (all to the closest 1/32-inch), and even cam orientation. Once this is all recorded, and anything changes, you'll know if string creep occurs. With a few twists of the bowstring and/or cables, your set-up will regain its original settings.

Some archers prefer to make small marks using a paint marker along the bow's cams, denoting proper cam orientation. If the cam-position moves, then you know string creep has occurred. Personally, I tend to etch marks into the cams (using the end of a knife or nail) to protect them from rain, snow, or other outdoor elements.

Bowstrings require constant service. Do your best to clean the fibers and apply quality string wax regularly, which protects them from heat, moisture and other elements that can cause string stretch or creep.

Also, no serious bow mechanics leave their arrow fletching to a pro shop. Fletching damage is constant and can be quite costly to repair time and again. Doing your own fletching also allows you to maintain better quality control, which is important, since keeping your overall arrow weight and fletching orientation consistent improves accuracy.

Basic Tasks

As a home bow mechanic, you should know how to press a bow, remove and inspect cams and axles, examine and replace bowstrings (when necessary), tie in a peep sight, apply center serving, create a strong release loop, wax bowstrings, align arrow rest center-shot, paper tune arrow flight, and build and fletch arrow shafts. All of these tasks are fairly rudimentary once the task becomes familiar.

One of the most important tricks of the trade is to learn how to tie serving and the appropriate finishing knot. Once you learn this, you can apply center serving, tie in a peep sight or your arrow rest's pull-down cord. This is a must, in my opinion, because these are the elements that can break or loosen at the worst times—even while you're miles away from your car in the back country. With the knowhow you can remedy such problems in a pinch and with great ease.

Applying New Center Serving: The process of tying on center serving is tough for the beginner. However, with a bit of trial and error, anyone can learn it. And once you do, you won't forget for life. The best way to learn is to have a friend show you. If no one is available, then practice using a thick nylon cord and a wooden dowel until the process is ingrained.

In simple terms, here's how to do it.

Step 1: Mark the position of the where the center serving meets the unserved portion of the bowstring by rubbing a line here with a marker pen. Next, carefully remove old center serving by cutting away at the edges using a semi-sharp knife. Once a few of the wraps are cut, the serving should begin to unravel. (Exercise extreme caution here, being careful not to damage or cut the actual bowstring.) Remove center serving entirely.

Step 2: Place the bow in a press and compress the limbs so the strings are relaxed. Grab hold of the bowstring and separate the strands evenly (i.e., with a 20-strand string, split it so there are 10 strands to a side) right where it was rubbed up with the marker pen. Then, insert a 12-inch tag of center serving thread. Un-press the bow so the bowstring is taut. The pressure now will hold the threaded tag in place.

Step 3: Then, disconnect the cable guard if necessary, and strap away cables using a soft nylon cord to free the area for serving.

Step 4: Next, wrap serving around bowstring tight and continue to serve over the top of the tagged end until you have about 6 inches of serving, then trim the tag if any remains, and serve another 10 turns or so. While serving, it helps to hold the tag end tight and parallel to the bowstring as you serve, otherwise it has a tendency to wrap around the string during serving.

Step 5: The next step is the confusing part. You need to draw out about 2 feet of thread and form a large loop. Next, begin serving inside the loop from the bottom of the loop up. Serve in the same direction as before. Make 20 wraps.

Step 6: Finally, lay the end of the serving (and jig) along the top of the loop and continue serving down by twisting the loose loop section with your hand. Once the bottom serving is completely unraveled, pull the serving end tight (by grasping the jig and pulling) and trim off. The serving is now complete.

My favorite center serving material is BCY's Halo and Brownell's Crown when using a fingers release. I prefer BCY 62XS or Brownell Diamondback serving with a release-aid and using a string loop since it lays flatter and grips the bowstring better. Both 62XS and Diamondback servings have a slight blend of polyester, and seem to hold a string loop more in place over Halo or Crown.

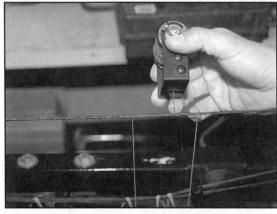

A special knot is necessary to secure a center serving. Form a large loop and then begin serving inside the loop, but this time back up toward the serving you just laid. Once this is done, serve by hand back over the loose tag end, then cinch it tight.

BCY's #62XS is one of the best materials for center serving.

BY JOE BELL

Which Loop Should You Use?

There are various types of string loops, and each offers certain advantages. I asked pro archer John Dudley for his thoughts on the various types of loop arrangements. This is the feedback he offers.

Style 1: Single Nockset with D-Loop

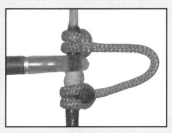

PROS: With one tie-in nockset below the arrow nock, this arrangement creates constant downward pressure to the arrow during the launch cycle and puts the release jaw directly behind the arrow nock. Depending on the bow and arrow rest, this can sometimes produce better accuracy. This configuration is good for bows using a cam ½ or hybrid system.

CONS: Dudley says the downside to this method is that if the loop breaks, you lose the exact location of the top nockset (or nock point in this case), and the bow's precise tune. Also, if the loop knot is not truly uniform or round it can place various pressures on the arrow nock, affecting consistency. However, renowned target archer Dave Cousins uses this loop set-up so obviously it works.

Style 2: Double Nockset with D-Loop

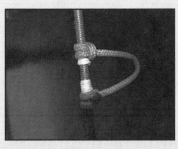

PROS: This is Dudley's favorite set-up, since it creates a uniform nocking point so that you never lose your bow's tune, despite loop replacement or loop length adjustment. This is a configuration that has worked very well with single cam bows.

CONS: Lack of downward arrow pressure on the rest. If your arrow lifts up off the rest, despite sufficient "gapping" between the arrow nock and bottom tied-in nockset, then stick with Style 1.

* There is also a slight variation to this system that combines the benefits of system 1 as well as system 2. Tie a top nocking point that is about one-third the size of the bottom nocking point (as shown in photo).

Style 3: Single Nockset with Loop Under

PROS: This set-up works well with archers that prefer lower anchor points. Also, this loop style places a lot of downward pressure on the arrow, resulting in excellent accuracy. Also, since the loop is narrow, it allows for greater string torque without affecting bowstring movement. This results in a more forgiving set-up.

CONS: This loop is slower to hook up in a hunting situation, and is recommended only for narrow release hooks.

Note: When placing a tie-in nockset below the arrow nock, Dudley recommends leaving 1mm gap between the nock and nockset, since at full draw the gap at these points will close because of the string's angle. This alleviates the nockset from pinching the arrow nock and affecting accuracy.

As a rule of thumb the bottom nocking point should never be smaller than the top nocking point.

Dudley, after tying in the nocksets, likes to verify that there isn't a pinching problem. He does this by unscrewing the field point from the arrow, loading it on the string, and then coming to full draw. If the arrow lifts up off the rest, the bottom tied nockset is too close to the arrow nock. When the arrow stays on the rest during the entire draw cycle (identifying proper downward pressure), he then knows the placement of the nockset is perfect.

Fact: Learn how to do center serving; it's the most important task of all.

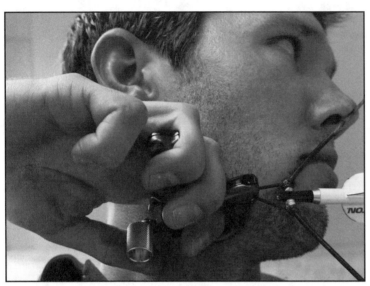

You can create any size string loop you want, but the author recommends at least ½-inch of room between the string and loop. This allows ample clearance for the release's nose.

More so than anything, a self-bow mechanic can customize his center serving for appropriate nock fit. By not doing this, you're opening the door to inconsistent shooting.

All these center serving materials come in various diameters to match the throat of your arrows' nocks, although I favor .024, .025 or .026-inch diameters for a slightly snugger nock fit. However, at times I may use .021 or .022-inch diameters. It simply depends on the thickness of the bowstring and shape of the nock's throat.

Using String Loops: String loops, or D-loops, provide many advantages. For starters, they allow the arrow's nock to stay vertically consistent as the arrow cycles through the bow. Slow-motion photography has shown arrow nocks that aren't supported above and below the nock often tend to "string walk" down the string, or back and forth. This wrecks accuracy.

Secondly, string loops are flexible, thus they provide a more forgiving shot, which results in better arrow flight.

And finally, they free the bowstring and center serving from unjust wear and damage. These, in my opinion, overpower a loop's only disadvantage, which is a slight loss in draw length and speed.

Making a string loop is pretty straightforward. Start with good loop material. BCY and Brownell material is what I use. I like 2mm thickness, or .078-inch thick.

Loop size is dependent on many things. The type of nocks, release and in smaller part the anchor style you use.

I like a fairly short loop to maximize draw length. To increase accuracy further, I usually mark the nock height and nock thickness on the bowstring, and then I tie in a top and bottom nockset using serving thread. Then I tie in my D-loop above and below these points. I tie most of my loops with a 4 ¼-to-4 ½-inch size cord, complete with burned ends.

How to Make the Loop: To start, take a piece of cut nylon loop material and broom the ends by smashing the edges with your finger. Then using a pocket lighter, burn the edges, all the while twisting the end over the flame. Then blow the flame out as a ball forms. These beads will prevent the loop from untying on the bowstring.

This is the proper way to install a string loop.

Now, attach the loop material to the bowstring by folding it in half (to form a loop) and then by grasping the beaded edges looping them around the string. Pull one beaded end and cinch one end onto the serving. Look at how the knot is formed. By looking at the knot, this should help you tie a knot on the other side in identical fashion. *(Note:* Be sure to tie the knot so the beaded end is pointing in the opposite direction as the other.)

To secure the loop for shooting, attach your release and give it a few firm tugs (without drawing the bow!) Once this is done, you can draw back on the bow fully to completely tighten and secure the loop. To adjust the loop up or down, simply revolve it and it will move up or down the center serving.

Smash the ends of the loop material with your finger to form a mop-like bundle. Then, twist the cord with your fingers as you burn the end. Doing so will form "balls" at each end, which is necessary to keep the loop from untying on the bowstring.

Taking It to the Next Level

An arrow cut-off saw, arrow-speed chronograph, arrow straightner and/or spine tester, arrow spinner, bow vise, and digital grain scale are a few more essentials you can add.

Personally, I recommend an arrow-cut off saw to all levels of bow mechanics. At times, you may have to experiment or help buddies with arrow lengths and traveling to a pro shop for this simple procedure can be a major inconvenience, not to mention a costly endeavor over time. I bought my basic Apple arrow-cutting tool about 20 years ago, and it's still going strong after relentless cutting of my own, as well as my friends' arrows.

A good bow mechanic will use a variety of tools to handle simple archery chores. This Easton digital draw-weight scale is handy for maintaining a precise bow tune.

TECH TIPS

Wax Up!

Waxing bowstrings regularly lubricates, extends the life, and prevents water absorption from reaching the string's fibers—all which can negatively affect performance. Take a top-quality wax such as BCY's ML-6, and apply it liberally to the string. Next, using your fingers, rub in the wax quickly (so it softens and penetrates into the fibers) and wipe away excess. Perform as frequently as you can, but no less than every two-to-three weeks. Just so you know, there's no such thing as overwaxing a bowstring; you can only under wax.

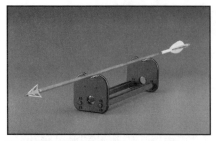

Pine Ridge makes a great arrow spinner, which is useful to ensure proper broadhead concentricity.

A digital bow scale is important to maintain consistent arrow weight by measuring each arrow component as well as total arrow weight.

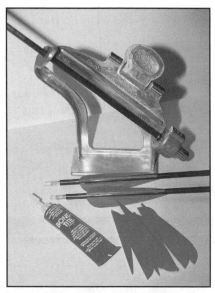

Build your own arrows, for obvious reasons. It's cheaper, more convenient and allows you to maintain consistency, so each arrow is the same. This increases accuracy. The author prefers the Bitzenburger jig, because of its quality design and heavy-duty construction.

TECH TIPS

How to Make a Tie-In Nockset

For tie-in nocksets, use small, resilient serving material, such as BCY 3D or 2S. Make these nocksets about 1/8-inch thick or so.

To make a nockset, simply make a basic overlapping knot (like you would to start the knot on a shoe lace) then do the same on the underside of the bowstring. Continue this over/under arrangement of knots (be sure to form the knots in the same fashion each time to create a clean/uniform knot). Do this several times until you reach the correct length.

I usually end my serving at this point by loosening the last knot. Then I take an extra piece of thread, form a loop with this thread, and then place it through the "eye" of the last knot. The extra-thread loop is now across where the arrow nock would be. Now, I tighten the knot, then form one additional knot on the underside of the string. From here, I take the tag ends of the serving and insert them through the extra-thread loop. I hold both tags and pull on the ends of the extra-thread loop, so that it draws the serving through the knot and secures them. Tighten, trim excess, and burn the ends flush to the serving.

The method preferred by pro archer John Dudley is to actually continue to serve (instead of ending the serving on the last knot) and back track your over/under knots along the serving that was first laid out. When you get to the end where you first began, backtrack again for two over/under knots, and tie a double knot. Then cut the excess and burn the ends flush to the knots.

One item perhaps all archers should own is an arrow-spinning tool. Pine Ridge makes a great model, and it's even easily disassembled for travel. This tool allows you to revolve arrows at high speeds so you can quickly identify critical "wobble" that often occurs where the broadhead base or ferrule meets the shaft's insert or end. Movement in this area means the broadhead is not seated completely flush and will create unwanted air friction in flight. For the best accuracy, no wobble should occur. *(Note:* Some movement in the tip area of the broadhead usually doesn't affect accuracy since the tip is too small to create air drag and affect flight.)

Beyond all that, becoming your own bow mechanic is truly rewarding, just as it is when you can make repairs to your car, truck, home or boat. There's a sense of pride and satisfaction in it that comes only from doing it on your own. This makes you even more proficient as an archer, and it makes the archery experience that much better.

Third-Axis Leveling

Most of today's bow sights come with a bubble level that is mounted perpendicular to the sight pins. This is called second-axis leveling, and helps you achieve consistent shooting, particularly on side-hill shots.

However, third-axis leveling, on those sights that have this feature, is crucial when shooting uphill or downhill. Third axis is the horizontal adjustment of the sight pins and/or housing (think of the pins/housing pivoting toward or away from you).

At full draw is the best way to level your sight's third axis since you can incorporate the natural torque involved in holding the bow. The simplest, most effective way to level the third axis of your sight is to create a vertical reference on your sight guard. You can make a vertical aiming wire on any sight by taping a piece of thread atop the guard (as close to horizontal center as possible), and affix a washer at the other end of the thread so it dangles downward. Hold your bow so that the bubble reads level, wait for the weight not to dangle then tape the other end of the string in place. You now have a plumb aiming wire.

Next, to adjust the third axis: 1. Hang a plumb bob from the ceiling or door jam. 2. Now draw your bow and aim with the wire up or down at about a 45-degree angle on the plumb bob. Make the necessary adjustments until the bubble reads level, which is your third-axis leveling. You're done—simple.

Bowstring Questions and Answers

By Mike Slinkard, *President, Winner's Choice Bowstrings*

Question: What kind of serving do you recommend for tying in peep sights?

Answer: I normally use a small material like BCY 3-D. I do a series of overhand knots around the string above the peep about ½-inch in length, leaving 6-inch ends when I am done. I then do the same thing below the peep except maybe just a little shorter, and I cut and burn off the ends on this one (be sure not to burn the string itself).

I then push both knots toward the peep until they are in a close and snug position. Then I take the 6-inch ends from the top loop and go around each side of the peep using two turns above and two below on each string side. Then I tie a few more overhand knots below the bottom knot. This just keeps everything together. You can still adjust the peep location slightly by "inch worming" the knots and peep up and down if you need to. There are a lot of other good ways to do this, but I like this way best because it is solid but still slightly adjustable.

Question: How often should you change out bowstrings? How do you detect wear? Is three years too long to shoot a 450 or 452 material bowstring?

Answer: The old standard is once a year, but for most shooters they can go much longer as long as they are using a premium string that does not have serving separation issues (Winner's Choice are guaranteed against this for 1 year).

With our strings, some key things to pay attention to would be that when sudden serving separation, creep or peep rotation does occur, this is the first clue that strands are weakening and should be replaced. Of course, any broken or excessively worn strands may also demand string replacement. Today's fibers last extremely long as long as they are maintained well with high quality string conditioner. We have seen many of our strings go in excess of 5 years on bows that are used for normal hunting situations with no problem. As with anything, use and proper care are the big factors in string life.

Question: What serving material do you recommend for tying in nocksets?

Answer: I use either BCY 3-D serving or the small-diameter BCY Halo.

Question: With string silencers such as Sims, do you recommend serving them in place with dental floss? Or is this not necessary?

Answer: I serve mine in just to be certain that they cannot move up or down the string. Accuracy problems will result with any string accessory that does not stay in a consistent position.

About the Author

Joe Bell was inflicted early on with the passion to bowhunt. As a young teen, he took up bowhunting big game and has never grown tired of the challenge, pursuit and mystique inherent in this great pastime. Today, at only 36, Bell has successfully meshed his enthusiasm for the sport with a career. After more than a decade of writing for the outdoor industry, serving as past associate editor of *Petersen's Bowhunting* and long-time editor of *Bow & Arrow Hunting* Magazine, he is living his childhood dream. As an industry professional, he has bowhunted the far reaches of the continent, harvesting a wide variety of big game. Admittedly, though, his true love is pursuing Western deer, elk and antelope. He is perhaps best known for his meticulous testing, reviewing and tuning of archery gear, which makes him well qualified to write this book.

Technical Bowhunting—Index